MW00804223

Student Teaching

Student Teaching

Past, Present, and Future

Leah Wasburn-Moses and Philo C. Wasburn

LEXINGTON BOOKS
Lanham • Boulder • New York • London

Published by Lexington Books
An imprint of The Rowman & Littlefield Publishing Group, Inc.
4501 Forbes Boulevard, Suite 200, Lanham, Maryland 20706
www.rowman.com

6 Tinworth Street, London SE11 5AL, United Kingdom

British Library Cataloguing in Publication Information Available

Library of Congress Control Number: 2020949051

ISBN 978-1-7936-0232-9 (cloth)
ISBN 978-1-7936-0233-6 (electronic)

Contents

Chapter 1

Origins of Student Teaching

FORERUNNERS OF STUDENT TEACHING

Throughout Europe, as early as the Middle Ages, some teacher training had already developed. The most common of these involved learning a trade by serving an apprenticeship, sometimes for as long as seven years, with a "master" teacher. Like contemporary student teaching, it was based on the fundamental premise that one learns by doing.

Beginning in the 1400s, more organized and extensive efforts were made in England, France, and Germany to train teachers by creating schools for this purpose. In these schools, students were given practice in teaching by having them teach demonstrations to their fellow students. Also embodying the concept of learning by doing, the schools included efforts to teach the future teachers "how to teach" (pedagogy) in addition to providing them with the necessary subject matter background (Johnson, 1968).

In the United States, teacher education programs were established more slowly in response to rapid population growth. Enactment of the "Old Deluder Law" by the Massachusetts legislature in 1647 represents one of the first efforts to establish state-supported schools (Stillwaggon, 2012). Most education was done by clergy or at least in connection with the church. The law assigned responsibility for education to the local community. However, its intent was explicitly religious. The law was to create a literate public so that "ye old deluder Satan" could not use illiteracy to "keep men from knowledge of ye scriptures." The Act required any Massachusetts town with more than fifty households to support a town teacher. Towns with more than 100 households were required to set up a grammar school for its children. In any town that failed to provide the required education, families had to pay a five pounds fine to a neighboring school for each year until the town installed its own teacher or school.

Prior to the 1830s, most childhood education in America occurred in children's family homes, in the workplaces of craftsmen, in tuition-based private schools, in free schools for paupers or in so-called Dame schools (Schneider, 2018). The last of these merits a separate, brief description because they first displayed several characteristics that came to define the conduct of public school education in this country.

Dame schools initially developed in Massachusetts and reflected the intent of the Old Deluder Act. They were small private schools usually taught in their homes by working-class women with limited opportunities for employment (Harper, 2010; Wyman, 1995). They later appeared throughout America but remained most common in New England, where literacy was expected by all social classes. This was not the case in the southern colonies where girls and nonwhites had fewer educational opportunities and where fewer educated women were willing to be teachers (Perlmann & Margo, 2001). In Dame schools, children were taught the alphabet and reading, as well as writing, spelling, grammar, arithmetic, geography, morals, and religious beliefs. There was no regulation of the specific content or quality of the instruction. Aspiring teachers simply had to satisfy school officials and parents that they had completed a level of schooling beyond that of which they proposed to teach and that they would maintain order in the classroom. The major qualification for teaching was being appointed by a local authority (Cuban, 1984).

PIONEERS

Samuel Read Hall was among the first to be effective in publicly expressing the need to vastly increase not only the number of public or common schools but also schools with formal programs to train teachers so as to improve the quality of instruction in these institutions. While there had been previous sporadic attempts to train teachers in the United States, Hall's school signaled the beginning of including practical teaching in this country (Johnson, 1968, p. 189). Born in New Hampshire in 1796, Hall was a clergyman and educator. In 1823 he established the Concord Academy, the first training school for teachers to be recognized in the United States. He helped organize the American Institute of Instruction, the oldest educational association in this country, in 1830. That year he also became principal of a new teachers' seminary at Phillips Academy in Andover, MA. Subsequently, Hall directed the Homes-Plymouth Academy in Plymouth, NH in 1834, and the Craftsbury Academy in Craftsbury, VT, in 1840, to which he added a teacher training department.

Hall's Concord Academy may represent the introduction of student teaching into U.S. teacher training programs. Previously, teacher training focused on the memorization of textbook material and recitation. To this was added practical teaching experience done under the close supervision of an experienced teacher. Also common was the practice of requiring students to write "knowledge papers" for their supervising teachers during this experience to prove their mastery of the subject matter to be taught. They also wrote lesson plans and papers on the needs of each pupil in their practice classroom.

Perhaps Hall's greatest influence was exercised through the 1829 publication of his *Lectures on School Keeping*, the first American book for both teachers and children. In the first chapter, he made this case for formal programs of teacher education:

Young gentlemen,

Without making the "science of teaching" a study, how can you be better prepared for success in it, than you would be to succeed in law or medicine, without having studied either? It is true that many have engaged in teaching without having gained any knowledge of the nature of their work save what they acquired in the schools in which they attended while children. But that others have pursued a course inconsistent and unreasonable is no reason why you should imitate their bad example, and thus render your labours useless, or even injurious, to the children placed under your care. A moment's attention to the subject, it would seem to me, sufficient to show that no one ought to assume the office of teacher without having endeavored first to obtain some correct views of the subject, of the obstacles in his way—the manner in which they may be overcome—the labour he is to perform—and the most probable means of benefitting, in the highest degree, his youthful charges. (Hall, 1829, p. 2)

Calvin Ellis Stowe, another early influential advocate of universal public education and teacher education, was born in Massachusetts in 1802. Like Hall, Stowe achieved prominence in his role as a religious educator. A professor of Biblical Studies at Lane Theological Seminary in Cincinnati, Ohio, he contributed to the development of Cincinnati's College of Teachers.

The 1820s, 1830s, and 1840s were periods of substantial growth in America's urban population and its rate of immigration. In 1820, 9.6 million lived in urban centers. By 1830 that population has risen to 12.9 million, and by 1840 it numbered 17.1 million. For the 1820s decade, the rate of immigration more than doubled, and between 1830 and 1840 it more than tripled. By 1850, in some states, such as Massachusetts, which became a center of growth for inclusive public education, the foreign born constituted more than 16% of the population. In response to this demographic change, Stowe warned that "unless we educate our immigrants, they will become our ruin.

It is no longer a question of benevolence, of duty, or enlightened self-interest
. . . but of self-preservation" (Travers, 1969, p. 83).

Some popular support for the creation of a system of common schools
already existed. Many workers envisioned the schools as potentially promoting opportunities for their children. One favored proposal noted that schools
could allow children to study part of the day and work part of the day. This
would make it possible for them to continue their contribution to their family's income while receiving an education that would greatly enhance their
chance for social mobility.

In 1836 Stowe sailed to England to purchase a library for Lane Seminary.
Alerted to his trip, the Ohio State legislative officially appointed him as
an agent to investigate the public schools of Europe, particularly those of
England and Prussia. Upon his return, Stowe expressed his admiration of the
Prussian system of public education:

> The kingdom of Prussia, at the present time, affords the rare spectacle of
> an absolute sovereign exerting all his power for the intelligence and moral
> improvement of his people. The government of Prussia, in which the voice of
> the king is everything, and the voice of the people nothing, has done more for
> the education of the whole people than has ever been done by any other govern-
> ment on earth. (Stowe, 1836, p. 19)

Apparently, Stowe did not fully appreciate the irony that one of the potentially most democratizing public institutions had been created by one of the
most totalitarian governments. He had discussed the issues raised by publicly
funded schools teaching specific religious doctrines. He failed to comment
on the political/ideological ends in which schools might be made to serve.

In 1837, Stowe presented his *Report on Elementary Instruction in Europe*
to the Ohio General Assembly. In his report, Stowe urged Ohio to adopt
a state-backed common school system. The legislature ordered a copy for
each of Ohio's school districts, and copies were given to state legislatures in
Massachusetts, Michigan, and New York.

Stowe's suggestion, while remarkably influential, was not without considerable criticism. As noted, his proposal was, to a large extent, a response to the
needs of America's rapidly expanding population. While, if adopted, it might
benefit the working class generally, some expressed concern that government-
funded schooling would result in higher taxes that would transfer money from
workers to support the education of the children from more prosperous families.
Various political, religious, and occupational groups objected that, by accom-
modating vastly expanding immigrant groups, publicly supported schools
would introduce "un-Protestant" values and modes of behavior into the society
and was contrary to the fundamental American principles of individualism

and Laissez-Faire (Lipset & Raab, 1970). Again, expanding school systems became a catalyst for growth in and reform of teacher education.

ESTABLISHING NORMAL

The idea of normal schools was derived from the French concept of the *Ecole normale*. This was a model school designed to teach standard teaching practices or the "norms" of teaching, which could be taught and learned like any other established discipline. The concept, emerging from the French Revolution, envisioned the development of a new body of teachers trained in the critical spirit and secular values of the Enlightenment. This would help ensure that quality education would be available to all. The peasant classes in France had remained largely illiterate well into the nineteenth century (Grew & Harrigan, 1990).

In America, normal schools developed to provide this burgeoning number of common schools with appropriately skilled teachers. Before their advent, most teachers simply attended elementary schools and subsequently returned to their schools as teachers. The major qualification for teaching was being recognized by a local authority. It was not until the beginning of the twentieth century that state licensing and certification requirements would be used as a means of upgrading teacher training (Tyack, 1967).

The first state-supported school for the exclusive purpose of training teachers opened in Lexington, Massachusetts, in 1839. The most widely recognized advocate of normal schools, Horace Mann, declared at the dedication of a school building in Bridgewater, MA, in 1846:

> Neither the art of printing, nor the trial by jury, nor a free press, nor free suffrage can long exist, to any beneficial and salutary purpose, without schools for the training of teachers; for, if the character and qualifications of teachers be allowed to degenerate, the free schools will become pauper schools, and the pauper schools will produce pauper souls, and the free press will become a false and licentious press, and ignorant voters will become venal voters, and through the medium and guise of Republican forms, an oligarchy of profligate and flagitious men will govern the land. (Quoted in Harper, 1939, p. 21)

Mann was born in Massachusetts in 1796. He studied at Litchfield Law School and was admitted to the bar in Dedham, MA, in 1822. Five years later, he was elected to the Massachusetts legislature as a member of the antislavery wing of the Whig Party. In this position, he expressed particular concern with public charities, funding the state's infrastructure, and, most vigorously, building and improving common schools.

In 1837, Mann was appointed Secretary of the State Board of Education. He continued to advocate for nondenominational, tax-supported public education that was to be available to all children regardless of their gender, religious, economic, or racial identities. He contended that, if sufficient in number and staffed by properly educated teachers, public schools would promote "social harmony" in many ways (Cremin, 1957). This was a focal concern in America throughout the nineteenth century.

More specifically, Mann contended that, being available to all, schools would enhance the opportunities for social mobility. This opportunity would be especially helpful to women, who faced very limited occupational possibilities and who might find positions as teachers. Further, public schools would produce a better educated and therefore more productive workforce and a better informed and more involved citizenry.

As a result of the efforts of Mann and the other common school advocates, free public education at the elementary level was available to most American children by the end of the nineteenth century. Massachusetts passed the first compulsory school attendance laws in 1852, followed by New York in 1853. By 1918 all states had passed laws requiring children to attend at least elementary school (Butts, 1978). However, the quality of the education they received in these schools varied greatly. As late as 1898, no more than one-quarter of the teachers had graduated from normal schools (Tyack, 1967).

There were several populations that did not fully support the common school movement, as discussed by Mann. Mann had argued that while the words and moral teachings of the Bible, such as the work ethic and obedience to authority, would be included in the public school curriculum, the schools were "secular institutions not theological seminaries." While his view reflected the beliefs and values of the liberal, middle class of New England, it was not favorably received by many Catholic and other religiously conservative groups in New England and elsewhere in the country.

In the mid-1840s, religious conflict surrounding public education was particularly intense. While Mann expressly intended public education to be fundamentally secular and nonsectarian, apparently he did want schools to make some use of the King James Version of the Bible. In large eastern cities, such as New York and Philadelphia, tensions arose between nativist and immigrant groups due, in part, to a rumor that Catholic immigrants would remove the Protestant Bible from the classroom curriculum (McMaster, 1910, p. 376).

As a result of the efforts of Mann and the other common school advocates, free public education at the elementary level was available to most white, male children by the end of the nineteenth century. Massachusetts passed the first compulsory school attendance laws in 1852, followed by New York in 1853. By 1918 all states had passed laws requiring children to attend at least elementary school, although there were significant differences in their statements, interpretations, and enforcement of the laws. Also, Catholic opposition to common schooling persisted and private Catholic schools were created. Religious conflict continued until 1925 when the U.S. Supreme Court ruled in *Pierce v. Society of Sisters* that parents had the legal option of sending their children to private rather than public schools (Butts, 1978).

For most of its history, access to elementary education has been limited to white children from relatively prosperous homes or has been racially segregated. In the northeast in the mid-1800s, the number of common and normal schools was increasing steadily. While there were no laws requiring racial segregation in the schools, it was often practiced. Generally, public funding for white schools was greater than that for black or predominantly black. This produced qualitative differences in schooling. Teachers in white schools were better prepared and generally received higher pay. School buildings were of better quality and textbooks were more up-to-date (Herbst, 1966; Orazum, 1982).

While public education and associated teacher education were advancing in the northern states, the majority of African Americans lived in the South. Here they received very little to no formal education before the Civil War. Until Lincoln issued the Emancipation Proclamation in 1863, less than 10% of blacks were literate. White opposition to African American success had resulted in only the most rudimentary of schools available to blacks. In so far as there was any support for black public schooling, it was argued that its funding was a responsibility of the federal government and acts of private philanthropy rather than local communities. Before the Civil War, no southern state had an established system of public schools. There were some common schools that white children could attend, but none that were organized and required by the state. Blacks had established a tradition of educational self-help. However, most were more concerned about equal opportunity than with mixed education (Pierce, 1955).

After the Civil War, Jim Crow laws in the southern states mandated a dual education system based on race. The relatively few schools available to blacks were grossly inferior. Most were similar to those available to black children in South Africa under Apartheid (Walker & Archung, 2003). Typically, they were overcrowded, and children of all age groups were taught together in a single classroom. Few books were made available. Those that were out-of-date and did not contain discussion of ideas such as freedom and equality, or that government should get its power from the consent of the governed.

Most Jim Crow schools taught their students only those skills that fit the needs of white society such as those required for agricultural work or domestic service. In rural areas of the South, where most blacks lived, schools were often scheduled around the cotton growing season and were open as little as two or three months a year. Children were often pulled out of school because they were needed on the farm to plant and harvest crops along with their sharecropper parents. Many left after fourth grade.

After the Civil War, Congress established the Freedmen's Bureau to extend federal authority to the defeated South. Before the creation of the Freedman's Bureau, some schools had been established by benevolent and religious societies. The Bureau cooperated with these organizations and with state authorities in establishing and maintaining schools until a common school system could be supported by the restructured local governments (Parker, 1954). The service of thousands of "schoolmarms" from the North who served as agents of the Freedmen's Bureau facilitated the development and operation of the common schools (Small, 1979).

Some normal schools did develop in the South. Primarily, these were to train teachers who could provide their students with the attitudes and labor skills needed by the region's economy and compatible with the values embedded in its social structures. Future teachers were to accept and preach an ethic of hard work and the "dignity of labor" (Anderson, 1988). Typically, completion of a four-year curriculum was not required for admission to the schools. Those who successfully completed the schools' courses did so "with an educational equivalent in quality to that of a fair tenth grade program" (Anderson, 1988, p. 35).

STUDENT TEACHING IN NORMAL SCHOOLS

Across the country, much of what constituted the curriculum of normal schools involved extensive training in the subjects that were the focus of the common schools in which the students were preparing to teach: reading, writing, spelling, geography, grammar, and arithmetic. Only after students had demonstrated mastery of these subjects would they be admitted to professional training. Work in this program typically "consisted of 13 weeks in the history of education, 27 weeks in the science of education, 31 weeks in the methods in the elementary branches, and 20 weeks in mental science, a week being defined as 45 minutes a day for 5 days" (Pangburn, 1932, p. 14). Practice teaching preceded by significant amounts of observation was also standard in normal schools.

The earliest student teaching under the normal school model was conducted at an onsite school, typically called a "model," "practice," or "training school," a forerunner of the "laboratory school." All of these terms are used interchangeably in the professional literature. By the early 1900s, each normal school had a training school grades K-8. These training schools were located in the same wing or the basement of the normal school. Each school had a director and assistants called critics who supervised student teachers. Critics were typically two-year normal school graduates. On average, there were ten teacher candidates for eight students in the training school. By 1920, student teaching in some form or another was a part of the great majority of teacher training programs.

However, there was great variation among schools in regard to the amount of practice required, the students used in these schools, and the quality of supervision provided for "practice teachers." Typically, requirements for "practice teaching" involved a minimum of two weeks. Even though onsite practice for student teaching and other field experiences remained common for a century, early criticisms included an atypical student population and that the community did not want their youth to be the subject of experiments (Johnson, 1968). The development and acceptance of the field of educational psychology in the late 1800s, with its emphasis on the learner, the learning process and teaching method, helped to establish direct experiences with students as one of the most valuable parts of teaching preparation (Johnson, 1968).

In 1929, a grant through the Carnegie Foundation resulted in a prominent study called the Commonwealth Teacher Training Study. This study examined the traits and activities of practicing teachers in order to determine objectives for teacher education programs. It explored difficulties encountered by teachers in their practice and the most effective ways to solve these programs. The report concluded that teacher training programs should either select teachers who possess these traits or develop them through schooling. Thus began the long-standing debate over whether teachers are "born" or "made" (Edelfelt & Raths, 1998).

While the curriculum presented above clearly focused on teacher training, until the turn of the century, normal schools were basically post-elementary schools that often competed with high schools for enrollment of students with general education goals or goals preparing for professions other than teaching school (Urban, 1990). However, concern over the curriculum of normal schools and lack of explicit tie-in with the profession of teaching dated back almost to the inception of the model. In 1869, a report stemming from the fifth annual meeting of the American Normal Association called for more uniformity in preparation due to the perceived lack of application of professional science in normal schools. The goal of this work was seen as necessary in order to elevate teaching as a profession. Twenty years later, another report made to the Department of Normal Schools set what can be seen as the first standards for teacher education, including admission requirements and "clinical experiences." In what is one of the first references to "student teaching," this set of standards states that "the number of children entrusted to a beginning student teacher should be small, approximately 10 or 12" (Edelfelt & Raths, 1998, p. 4).

ISSUES WITH THE NORMAL SCHOOL MODEL

Religiously based beliefs and prevailing economic conditions combined to establish that the majority of students attending normal schools would be women. Consequently, they also influenced, and continue to influence, major issues facing teachers. The quotation below, from 1849, clearly expresses dominant beliefs of that time:

> God seems to have made woman peculiarly suited to guide and develop the infant mind, and it seems . . . very poor policy to pay a man 22 to 40 dollars a month, for teaching children the ABCs, when a female could do the work more successfully at one third the price. (Littleton, MA School Committee, 1849)

While the explicit purpose of normal schools was to provide future teachers with technical training, they also gave instruction in academic subjects so that their students would be familiar with the topics that would be teaching. In rural areas, subjects might include agriculture, husbandry, and mechanical arts. This training was essential, for normal school students tended to come from less advantaged class backgrounds and whose schooling often was inadequate (Herbst, 1980).

Still, a high proportion of those who enrolled in normal schools did not intend to become teachers. Rather, their hope was to secure a secondary school education for themselves, at minimal cost. Many sought to leave their rural homes and qualify for urban employment beyond mill or factory work. Women often prepared to enter teaching as an easily attained occupation to engaged in before marriage and starting a family (Lucas, 1997).

Whatever their functions and perceived importance to the teaching profession, by 1898, normal school graduates still accounted for less than one-quarter of all teachers then employed nationwide (Lucas, 1997). Other agencies such as private academies, Latin grammar schools, and the growing number of public secondary schools all continued to provide all the training that generally was viewed as essential to the preparation of future teachers. Taxpayers and state government officials complained explicitly that normal schools were an unnecessary expense that, at best, largely duplicated the work of the better-established institutions. Many rejected the argument that normal schools were necessary to provide special training in abstract principles and techniques of teaching. Rather they maintained that "mastery of a body of subject matter, acquired by the example afforded by rigorous and systematic instruction was sufficient to confer that subject matter to others" (Lucas, 1997, p. 29). Practice teaching was not mentioned.

"It was obvious to nearly everyone at the end of the century that (normal schools) had fallen short of the ambitious hopes nurtured on them by the likes of Horace Mann. . . . What students got in normal schools was often little more than a brief review of the subject matter they were expected to teach plus some introduction to pedagogy and a smattering of advice on school discipline and classroom management" (Lucas, 1997, p. 30). Until the turn of the twentieth century, normal schools were basically post-elementary schools widely perceived to be inferior to the public high schools with which they competed for enrollment of older students (Herbst, 1980).

Over time, admission standards of normal schools became somewhat more demanding. The length of their courses increased by one year in 1839 to two years by 1860. Student teaching became part of this movement to make a profession of teaching (Harper, 1939). As the number of normal schools increased, so too did the number of colleges and universities that offered courses in topics such as the philosophy of education and teaching methods based on the developing fields of psychology and sociology. The latter development ultimately would lead to the demise of the normal schools and their eventual replacement by competing college- and university-based schools of education. This significant shift in responsibility for teacher education would enhance considerably the quality of training and the status of educators.

In conclusion, student teaching in the United States developed in concert with population growth and the growth of the public school concept. Pioneers in teacher education were strong advocates of the development of public education and saw teacher training as necessary to support these ends. Normal schools developed in the 1800s in order to provide growing schools with teachers and some degree of training, both in the north and, to a lesser extent, in the south. "Practice schools" within normal schools provided hands-on training that could be considered the forerunner of today's student teaching. Although normal schools represented the first attempt at widespread teacher education, they felt short of their goals, and critics began looking at other options to educate teachers.

Chapter 2

Evolution of Student Teaching

TEACHER EDUCATION IN TRANSITION

Toward the end of the nineteenth century, rapid population growth, urbanization, and technological change created an even greater demand for teachers at both the elementary and high school levels, increasing from about 20,000 in 1900 to more than 200,000 by 1930 (Borrowman, 1936, p. 129). In response, many normal schools began developing more elaborate curricula and increased the length of teacher education programs from two to four years, including increased time devoted to "practice teaching," typically conducted in onsite "model" or "training schools," as discussed in chapter 1. As early as the 1870s, normal schools had begun to transition into degree-granting teachers colleges.

By 1879 President J. C. Gilchrist of Iowa State Normal already had presented the arguments in favor of the "teachers college" degrees:

1. A system of professional degrees will make teachers prominent in society as a learned class.
2. A wise system of degrees securing some privileges and emoluments will prove a strong incentive in obtaining professional qualifications.
3. A system of degrees for teachers will induce a more perfect development of educational philosophy and pedagogical practice.
4. A system of degrees will make for more permanency in the profession (Quoted in Harper, 1939, p. 134).

By 1890, the number of traditional single-purpose normal schools had begun to decline. They eventually disappeared by the 1940s. Most had long suffered a reputation for low admission standards and inferior academic quality. Overall, normal schools had failed to provide a reliable supply of well-trained teachers for the nation's public elementary and high schools. It remains difficult to explain exactly which successfully transformed themselves into the four-year colleges, or why or how they were successful (Lucas, 1997).

While some of the emerging state teachers colleges evolved from normal schools, others were built from the ground up. Among the earliest of the state teachers colleges were those at Cedar Falls, Iowa; Albany, New York; and Ypsilanti, Michigan. By 1910 there were about a dozen in existence. Their number increased rapidly to approximately 50 by 1920 and about 150 by 1930 (Lucas, 1977, p. 55). By 1940, state teachers colleges were producing close to 60% of all public school teachers entering the field (Butts and Cremin, 1953, p. 604).

The primary reasons for the initial success of state teachers colleges are clear. They offered more diversified programs with greater academic rigor than did the normal schools. They began awarding degrees, which increased occupational opportunities and resulting chances for social mobility for their students. They came to operate as a local, affordable, and accessible form of higher education (Labaree, 2004).

The factors which had contributed to the rapid rise of state teachers colleges subsequently led to their decline and replacement by schools or departments of education within American colleges and universities. Not only did these programs offer much more systematically organized and academically informed curricula than did the teachers colleges, the degrees they offered bestowed much greater prestige and employment opportunities for their students. Furthermore, they produced far more teachers, for whom there was increasing demand, than did the state teachers colleges.

In 1862, Congress passed the first Morrill Land Grant Act. This was the first time the federal government became directly involved in support of higher education. The act provided for the establishment of an institution in each state to educate its citizens in the fields of agriculture, home economics, industrial arts, education, and other professions. Their schools of education vastly increased the number of students participating in advanced teacher training programs. Many of these future teachers previously had been excluded on the basis of their social class or race. A second Morrill Land Grant Act was passed in 1890. This act primarily sought to ensure further that no state could use race as a consideration in determining access to its land grant colleges.

During this period of transition from the normal school standard to teachers colleges to the integration with public and private colleges and universities, student teaching took many different shapes. Although the normal school had established "practice teaching," liberal arts colleges and private colleges did not always see the value of hands-on work with students, preferring to focus instead on coursework, as described above. Although universities did establish "model schools" after seeing their value, private colleges developed their practice teaching much later (Johnson, 1968). When student teaching took place in the model or practice school, supervision was conducted by practicing teachers. However, student teaching began to move to public schools over time as the number of teacher candidates overwhelmed the number of K-8 students who could be housed onsite. In public schools, student teaching supervision became a shared function between the school and the supervising college or university (Edelfelt & Raths, 1998).

INFLUENCE OF ORGANIZATIONS AND POLICY

Teachers have always experienced low pay, low prestige, and little ability to determine their own professional standards of performance. They have formed organizations in efforts to establish some professional independence and to elevate popular perception of public education, and, more concretely, to influence state laws that would affect teacher salaries, state pension plans, and tenure. Historically, the most influential of these organizations has been the National Education Association (NEA). Founded in 1857 as the National Teachers Association, it held its first meeting in 1858. It became the NEA in 1870 when it merged with the American Normal School Association, the National Association of School Superintendents and the Central College Association. The NEA was chartered by Congress as a union in 1906; today, it is the largest labor union and professional interest group in the United States. The stated mission of the NEA remains

> to advocate for education professionals and to unite our members and the nation to fulfill the promise to prepare every student to succeed in a diverse and inter-dependent world. (NEA.org)

About 1920, several states began requiring student teaching as a condition for certification. By 1930, the majority of states required student teaching for their standard teaching certificate. In 1938, the American Council on Education created the short-lived Commission on Teacher Education, whose charge was to implement existing research in current programs. The Commission set standards in ten areas, including an attempt to regulate student teaching. Ten years later, the Committee on Standards and Surveys of the American Association of Teachers Colleges, the forerunner of today's American Association of Colleges for Teacher Education (AACTE), sent questionnaires to teacher training institutions with promising practices in order to apply research to practice. The report, School and Community Laboratory Experiences in Teacher Education, affirmed the importance of direct experience with youth (Edelfelt & Raths, 1998). This report was followed up by three conferences and a publication now known as the Flowers Report. The Flowers Report divided what we now know as field experiences into "Laboratory Experiences" and "Student Teaching." The report determined that laboratory experiences should be integrated into all four years of programming. It urged full-time student teaching, creating assignments for student teaching that fit both the context of the field and the needs of teacher candidates, and shared supervision by college faculty and cooperating teachers. This report can be seen as one of the first attempts to regulate student teaching nationally (Edelfelt & Raths, 1998).

In 1956, the National Council of Accreditation of Teacher Education was formed. Its 1957-1958 survey showed that 294 teacher preparation institutions had its accreditation. At that time, accreditation required an average of eight semester hours of student teaching for elementary majors and seven hours for secondary majors. These formal requirements finally established student teaching as a central component of teacher training programs and made the programs more formalized and consistent throughout the country (Johnson, 1967). This included their goals, practices, program lengths, and supervision standards. Shortly thereafter, the NEA established the National Commission on Teacher Education and Professional Standards, now known as the TEPS Commission. The Commission was given responsibility for advancing the profession of teaching through the development of standards. The resulting New Horizons for the Teaching Profession gave states responsibility for creating policy around certification and program approval. This set of standards advocated for multiple field experiences, including "an internship in addition to student teaching and other laboratory experiences" (Edelfelt & Raths, 1998, p. 9).

The work of these organizations encouraged the growth of state-level bureaucracy and policy. During the first half of the twentieth century, state departments of education developed and increased standard, formal requirements for teacher education. These requirements, specifying length and format of programs, replaced the traditional and widely varied teachers' examinations that were locally controlled and had dominated the provision of teaching licenses during the 1800s (Wilson & Youngs, 2005). In the 1930s, state policy made it possible for teacher training institutions to enter agreements to provide practice teaching in public schools, paving the way for a shift from the use of "practice" or "laboratory" schools to practical experiences in public schools (Johnson, 1968). However, by 1930, more than half of the states had no academic requirements for secondary teachers other than having graduated from a recognized college, and most secondary teachers were not even teaching in their major area of study. After World War II, however, despite seeing the most severe crises in teacher supply in the country to date, twenty-three states increased requirements for elementary teacher certification to a four-year degree (Wilson & Young).

STUDENT TEACHING IN A CHANGING LANDSCAPE

Popular and academic reservations notwithstanding, from the mid-1800s to the beginning of the new century, the number of colleges and universities having education schools had practically doubled, climbing to a total of about 250 before 1910. Such growth was possible because teacher education always has been influenced significantly by market forces that govern the supply and demand for available teachers. Economic factors continuously have worked largely independently from popular or professional assessments of student teacher quality (Peseau, 1990).

Incorporating teacher education programs into colleges and universities had significant benefits and costs for both the profession of education and for the institutions in which they were to operate. Association with higher education provided the teaching profession long-desired status and academic credibility, both of which carried exchange value. However, the profession lost some autonomy in shaping its education programs. College and University faculty and administrations were in positions to influence such matters as admission standards, course contents, graduation requirements, and even student teaching.

Education programs generated substantial economic profit for their host institutions. Departments and schools attracted large numbers of tuition-paying students. If schools could keep class sizes large and faculty salaries low, and if they could dispense with the need for the expensive laboratories, extensive libraries, and small seminars that drove up the cost of many of their other courses, teacher education programs could generate considerable profit for the rest of the university. That is, they could operate as a college's or university's "cash cow." Student teaching became particularly profitable, as students pay a full semester's worth of tuition to work off campus full-time, using neither class space nor instructors' time. In exchange, the college or university pays a nominal stipend to a (usually) part-time supervisor and cooperating teacher. In addition, teacher education programs enhanced public support for colleges and universities by further claiming social usefulness. However, by offering education courses, including student teaching, which commonly were viewed as academically weak, colleges and universities also ran the risk of damaging their own credibility and institutional status (Labaree, 2004).

By 1915, student teaching was fairly universal. A 1917 report divided what we now call "field experiences" into "observation" and "practice teaching." An average of 170 hours was devoted to "practice teaching," which may or may not equate to today's view of student teaching, or a full-time internship teaching youth in schools. The number of hours required for each varied widely across the country. A lack of uniformity in standards and supervision was seen as a challenge; however, "practice teaching" was typically required in the final year after instruction in methods (Johnson, 1968).

Again, most teacher training programs used their own training departments for practice teaching until the 1920s (Johnson, 1968). The 1920s saw a significant growth in off-campus practice teaching, and the use of campus schools decreased by 27%. Not only was this trend due to model schools being unable to accommodate a quickly increasing number of teacher candidates, but criticisms continued regarding the differences between the model school setting and a real-life classroom. A 1931 survey of practice teaching in private liberal arts colleges found that 61% offered it, and most of the rest were planning to do so shortly. Three-quarters required student teaching to be senior year, working with one class per day in the public schools. These numbers lagged significantly behind public institutions (Johnson, 1968).

DISCORD IN HOST INSTITUTIONS

In the early to mid-1900s, there was considerable pressure on many colleges and universities to develop teacher education programs. As noted earlier, in part, this growth was the result of a vast increase in the number of school-age children. However, it also reflected the fact that more young people were now seeking education beyond the elementary level to facilitate their full economic, political, and social participation in the emerging urban-industrial culture. Therefore, standards of teacher certification needed to be raised, and there was an increasing demand that teachers be actual college graduates who had practical teaching experience.

In response, the number of teacher preparation programs offered in colleges and universities dramatically increased. The primary impetus for this growth was unlike the concern for the quality of professional performance that prompted the evolution of schools of medicine, law and engineering (Borrowman, 1975). In the end, the numerical demand for teachers resulted in lower admission requirements for education programs. The profession itself lacked the equivalent of the established body of knowledge and practices that defined many other professions. Teaching also was a career largely sought by women in the context of a society in which they faced considerable discrimination. All of these forces working together meant that education programs in colleges and universities, and those associated with them, had lower status than that bestowed by most other academic programs. "It is never a healthy circumstance when people who are held in low esteem exercise dominant influence in an important sphere" (Hirsch, 1996, p. 69).

In spite of the efforts of the NEA and other professional organizations to promote the interests of American teachers, and regardless of the contributions of college- and university-based departments and schools of education, the general public still needed to be convinced that teacher training programs, at any level, were important and required significant financial support. In popular culture, the belief persisted that "great teachers are born, not made," and there is little more to teaching than knowledge of one's subject matter, experience, and perhaps such personality characteristics such as patience and a liking for young people. Thus, many saw college- and university-based education programs as largely irrelevant to the practical concerns of classroom teachers (Clifford, 1986).

Unfortunately, it was not only the mass public that needed to be persuaded that college- and university-based professional education programs had value. Trustees, administrators, and faculty of the colleges and universities in which they were developing had to be persuaded that education schools in general, and their student teaching program, in particular, had a sound and legitimate academic foundation. This movement involved demonstrating that all preparatory courses had reasonable intellectual content and were based on the sort of knowledge that defined a legitimate academic undertaking. To achieve this goal, schools introduced more demanding programs. New plans of study included subjects such as the historical development of modern education, comparative study of educational systems, special topics in the philosophy of education and critical principles underlying the art of teaching and governing (Lucas, 1997, p. 44).

However, the introduction of such course offerings largely failed to convince established faculties that what they now offered remained not much more than a program of instruction "pitched not much more above the secondary level and for students who might not otherwise have qualified for regular admission" (Harper, 1935, p. 39). The inability of schools of education to meet what might be understood as the incompatible beliefs and wishes of the mass public and those of college and university faculties endures in some form to this day.

Because of these widespread criticisms, accompanying the economic benefits to a college or university for incorporating a teacher education program was a risk to the school's institutional status. Such programs have had, and continue to have, low academic prestige. The degree of threat reflects the locations of the program's development. In regional state universities, many of which evolved from normal schools, education schools tend to focus on the preparation of future teachers and the development of current teachers. This "vocational orientation" is consistent with that many of their other departments. The presence of professional education programs does not detract from their reputation. Present examples of schools that developed from normal schools to teachers colleges to state colleges to state universities include the State University of New York at Albany; Millersville University of Pennsylvania; Minnesota State University, Mankato; Northern State University, DeKalb, IL, and State University, Montclair, NJ (Labaree, 2004, p. 303). By way of contrast, colleges and universities whose status rests on their academic reputations risk a loss for including education schools. Consequently, rather than focusing on teacher preparation, which includes student teaching, their primary efforts have involved scholarly research and graduate school programs. They tend to be educationally strong but professionally weak (Karabe, 2005). "Overall, schools tend toward one pole or the other in these terms, with relatively few occupying middle ground. . . . Today, regional state universities produce the large majority of the country's teachers and maintain a strong reputation for relevance to community concerns" (Labaree, 2004, pp. 202–203).

Colleges and universities whose status has always rested on their academic reputation risk a loss for including education schools. These are institutions that maintain high academic entrance requirements, receive large research grants and produce a disproportionate number of publications in professional journals (Labaree, 2004, p. 304). Present examples of elite institutions that, nevertheless, were early to add education schools include the University of Michigan, the University of Iowa, Columbia University (Teachers College), the University of Chicago, Stanford University, Harvard University, the University of California at Berkeley, and Ohio State University.

There always has been some faculty and administration opposition to teacher preparation programs in these more prestigious colleges and universities. For example: "After Teachers College was created in the late Nineteenth Century it was often said that 120th Street, which separates Teachers College from the rest of Columbia University, is 'the widest street in the world.' . . . The price of professionalism unfortunately was the split between pedagogy and the traditional disciplines of the liberal arts and sciences" (Ravitch, 2003, p. 1).

To reduce status threat, programs that were included in the elite schools were structured so that they were more academically demanding. They drew more heavily on academic fields such as anthropology, history linguistics, political science, psychology, and sociology, and emphasized empirical research on education as a cultural and social institution. However, the schools made this accommodation at the expense of their professional relevance. They distanced themselves from training and serving classroom instructors. Their academic and theoretical concerns were seen "as little interest to school-based practitioners as the work of the divinity school archaeologist was to the preacher laboring over his Sunday sermon" (Glazer, 1974, p. 351 quoted in Clifford & Guthrie, 1988, pp. 87–88). Such perspective was consistent with the increasingly popular and generally accurate view that "no thought of growing respectable by becoming an arts college can deter the modern teachers college from its historic path of pragmatism and its obligation to point out the road to progress for public education" (Harper, 1939, p. 150).

In 1900 there were approximately 230 American colleges and universities offering some form of teacher education programs. By 1930 that number had risen to 600, by 1950 to 1,200, and in the last third of the century, the total would climb to almost 1,400 (Lucas, 1997, p. 60). This represented almost 80% of all American colleges and universities and reflected the fact that, by 2000, teaching employed about 15% of all college graduates each year (Labaree, 2004, p. 300).

STUDENT TEACHING AT MID-CENTURY

As noted, the curricula of virtually all schools of education came to represent some sort of balance between academic and vocational instruction that includes student teaching. The accommodations vary considerably. However, there are several categories of course offerings found in almost all programs. First, there is instruction in the subject matter future teachers are to tutor. This usually includes literacy, mathematics, history, science, and social studies. Second, there are pedagogical courses such as teaching methods, curriculum planning and assessment, technology in education, and effective classroom management strategies. Third, there is provision of field experience, culminating in student teaching as the program's capstone experience. Required activities involved in the student teaching experience came to include observing, tutoring, writing reports on experiences, assessing student characteristics and behavior, operating instructional media and designing instructional materials (Guyton & McIntyre, 1990).

Starting in the 1950s, regional state universities began to produce the large majority of the country's primary and secondary school teachers. Their programs tended to emphasize the importance of the student teaching experience. The label "Student Teaching" had surpassed "Practice Teaching" in the professional literature, and student teaching tended to be a full-time experience preceded by professional coursework. "Model" or "Practice Schools" gave way to the label "Laboratory Schools," which were still common on campuses, even as student teaching placements (Johnson, 1968).

An increasing amount of academic credit was provided to the student teaching experience, and some included experience in multiple grade levels (Johnson, 1968). Passing student teaching determined in part whether an individual would be recommended for certification as a licensed teacher. The priority assigned to this component of the education school curriculum was consistent with the positive evaluations of numerous analysts of American education (Andrews, 1964; Appleberry, 1976; Conant, 1963; Guyton & McIntyre, 1990; Haring & Nelson, 1980; Nosow, 1975).

Student teaching at mid-century already looked much the way it does today, a required block of multiple weeks of in-the-field practice under the supervision of a cooperating teacher and university supervisor. Support for student teaching from the broader education community was solid, as succinctly stated by an education school graduate in the early 1960s that "the teacher learns to teach in the classroom, not within the covers of a book" (quoted in Koerner, 1963, p. 343). However, external forces in society were about to coalesce to bring student teaching and teacher education even more stability, uniformity, and growth, moving the profession into the next century.

In conclusion, the increased demand for teachers during the Industrial Revolution spurred growth and development in normal schools, including expanded "practice teaching." Due to a variety of factors, normal schools were replaced by teachers colleges, which offered inexpensive, accessible higher education to the masses. As teachers colleges were subsumed into departments at established colleges and universities, student teaching developed unevenly. "Practice schools" were quickly outgrown and student teaching moved to the public schools by the 1930s. National organizations and state policy supported the standardization of teacher education and by proxy, student teaching, despite widespread criticism of low standards and prestige from the higher education community as well as the general public. By mid-century, student teaching was universal and looked quite similar to today's model.

Chapter 3

Student Teaching in the Post-Sputnik Era

The 1960s saw a new wave of criticism of teacher education. After the launch of the Russian satellite Sputnik in 1957, the fear of falling behind in education on the world stage put a national spotlight on the entire U.S. educational system. Improving and standardizing curriculum nationwide called for more and better teacher education. The baby boom furthered this agenda by requiring more teachers overall (Yarger & Leonard, 1974).

Arguably, the two most influential critiques were written by James Koerner and James Conant. Both analyses criticized the low quality of teacher candidates as well as the credentials of their preparers, university faculty. They decried the lack of research and supporting methods for teacher education, and recommending jettisoning education coursework, making teacher preparation the responsibility of the university rather than that of education departments. These very public critiques put education departments on the defensive and helped give rise to a "science of education," research programs directed at determining the best ways to educate teachers. Some early constructs developed from this movement included microteaching, performance-based and competency-based teacher education, and an emphasis on learning skills through practice (Urban, 1990).

As education became more nationally directed, student teaching as increasing in uniformity in terms of both structure and expectations. In 1964, seven national agencies formed the Joint Committee on State Responsibility for Student Teaching. Its goal was to outline states' responsibility for the enterprise of student teaching and to offer recommendations for its future. The first report of the committee recommended sharing responsibility for student teaching across K-12 and higher education; establishing a formal structure for student teaching, including specified roles and qualitative criteria for all involved; and state-level legislation, leadership, and funding (JCSRST, 1966).

The committee's second report, "A New Order in Student Teaching: Fixing Responsibilities for Student Teaching," begins by stating that "student teaching is almost universally accepted as the most important segment of teacher preparation" and proposes a new way of conceptualizing student teaching that "includes not only practice, but diagnosis, analysis, and synthesis in complex situations" (JCSRST, 1967, p. 1). The authors again recommend a statewide plan for student teaching, citing the need to address common problems such as the dearth of quality placements and supervisors, and determining readiness for student teaching on the part of teacher candidates. Their detailed recommendations are lengthy, but include clarification of roles, delineating of standard, organization of the structure of student teaching, and rewarding key players with both recognition and financial support. One key recommendation involved developing a statewide advisory board on teacher education and state commissions on student teaching (JCSRST, 1967).

TEACHING CENTERS

Just as national opinion began to solidify and rally around the need for increased centralization and collaboration in support of student teaching, an important concept took shape that quickly became a national movement. Definitions of the centers vary so widely that authors tend to agree only on the diversity of the concept (Schmieder & Yarger, 1974; Smith, 1974). The 1990 Handbook of Research on Teacher Education defines it simply as "a school within a school district to which many preservice students report for field experiences," and supported by a full- or part-time faculty member responsible for staff development (Guyton & McIntyre, 1990, p. 579). Burke (1978) saw them as a voluntary cooperation between institutions and agencies for purposes of enhancing teacher education. The concept was further clarified by Hess in 1971, who identified five specific objectives for centers:

1. To provide wide and varied direct experiences for the student teachers;
2. To develop a program of both preservice and in-service education for teachers;
3. To develop the role of the education center, coordinator, representative of the state, the college, and the school system;
4. To clarify the roles of all other center personnel; and
5. To explore state department involvement in the education center.

The concept appears somewhat similar to today's Professional Development School, but the role of the state and other entities are different. Other definitions shed more light on the complexity of the teaching center. Schmieder and Yarger (1974) identified the major purpose was to improve instructional quality in classrooms and schools, supporting staff development and educational renewal. They define a center as "a place, in situ or in changing locations, which develops programs for the training and improvement of educational personnel . . . in which the participating personnel have an opportunity to share successes, to utilize a wide range of education resources, and to receive training specifically related to their most pressing teaching problems" (p. 6). They identify seven organization types of teaching centers, from informal, voluntary arrangements for single higher education—K-12 partnerships, to relationships among multiple institutions of higher education and other educational organizations. Some were even initiated and maintained by legislative mandate.

By 1974, teaching centers were considered to be at the forefront of educational change, "one of the most prominent of the cutting edges in educational reform" (Schmieder & Yarger, 1974, p. 9), and noted for their rapid growth and expansion. A 1973 national survey uncovered 600 of these centers, many of which were supported by federal grants. The authors of this comprehensive study underscored the impact of collaboration through "consortium arrangements," including not just K-12 schools, districts, and institutions of higher education, but also state departments of education, teacher associations, regional education service centers, and even community agencies. Staffing, funding, and the use of incentives varied widely across the country (Yarger & Leonard, 1974). These authors all saw teacher centers as paving the way for a revolution in teacher preparation, as well as contributing to increased quality for student teaching through what we call today, deep partnership.

1968 REPORT ON STUDENT TEACHING

In 1968, James Johnson of Illinois State University published results of a federally funded research project entitled "A National Survey of Student Teaching Programs." The study reports data from 847 institutions of higher education, representing a 76% return rate. Data collected included background information from the institutions and administrative structures of student teaching, as well as information on the student teaching triad (cooperating teachers, university supervisors, and student teachers). The results are summarized below using the same headings as the author.

General background of the institution. Just under two-third (61%) of responding institutions were private, and 36% public. Although the vast majority (93%) were regionally accredited, only 48% were nationally accredited through the National Council for the Accreditation of Teacher Education, which had been founded in 1954. The modal category for responding institutions' full-time enrollment was 1,000–2,999 (34%), with 34% of the institutions reporting that 26–50% of their undergraduates were enrolled in teacher preparation programs.

Administration of student teaching. With respect to the title of the person in charge of student teaching, 38% of institutions reported a "Director of Student Teaching," with 28% reporting a "Head, Education Department." A full 27% used another title, though. Modal number of years in position was five to ten, with 26% of respondents. Few of these individuals devoted 100% of their time just to student teaching, however, most common responses were 11–25% of their time (28% of institutions) and 26–50% (24% of institutions).

Much space was devoted to the requirements of student teaching. Overall, 82% of institutions reported that elementary student teaching took place off-campus, as opposed to an in on-campus laboratory school. Sixty-five percent required full-time student teaching, with an average of just under eight credit hours for a mean length of 12 weeks and mean clock hours of just under 300. For secondary student teaching, only 60% required full-time with marginally fewer weeks (11.9) and 266 hours. Most student teaching took place in public schools (62%), and 30% reported a mixture of public and private. The rest were private schools only, campus laboratory schools, and "other." Although 23% of respondents reported having a campus laboratory school, most appeared not to use it as a placement for student teaching. Thirty percent of institutions allowed for summer student teaching.

Admission requirements for student teaching were fairly complex, including overall academic record (96% of institutions of higher education), record in major field (82%), record in education courses (77%), advisor recommendation (72%), emotional stability (65%), English proficiency (60%), physical fitness (60%), speech and voice (57%), and personal/social/ethical fitness (57%). Despite these multiple requirements, institutions reported denying a few applicants admission to student teaching, with few denying more than 3%.

With respect to the student teaching budget, 32% of institutions were able to provide figures, and the average cost for student teaching was $149 ($1,138 in 2019 dollars). Thirty-eight percent assessed a fee for student teaching, and the mean amount was $43 ($328 in 2019 dollars). Forth institutions reported receiving a student teaching research grant in the past two years, with a mean amount of $61,430 ($469,096 in 2019 dollars). Interestingly, the author lamented the scarcity of these grants in his conclusions.

The college supervisor. Institutions of higher education reported having about five full-time and nine part-time student teaching supervisors. The majority reported supervisors with masters or doctoral degrees; 31% of institutions had supervisors primarily with doctoral degrees. About 31% of all student teachers were supervised by graduate students. The modal number of student teachers assigned to each full-time supervisor was 16–20 (28%), with modal number of visits every one to two weeks (45%). The most common characteristics sought in college supervisors were human relations skills (45%), a knowledge of teaching methodology (29%), and a commitment to supervision (20%).

The student teachers themselves. Overall, in 91% of institutions, student teachers had prior classroom experiences in which they had been observed. Most (72%) allowed some choice in the student teaching assignment, with 75% providing an opportunity to teach at a "disadvantaged school." They spent 56% of their time in "actual teaching," with 20% observation and 24% participation. About 26% of responding institutions reported 1% or more of their student teachers failed their first assignment, although only 92% of these gave some type of second chance. Overall, most institutions (57%) reported eliminating less than 1% of their student teachers due to failure, and 23% eliminated none. Major causes of student teaching failure included "inability to control students" and "unwillingness to work." About 22% of institutions placed student teachers through the student teaching center discussed previously in this chapter.

Respondents were asked about the extent to which they used the following "Innovations": videotape equipment, tape recorders, microteaching, simulation, Flander's Interaction Analysis, Tabas's Teaching Strategies, Bloom's Taxonomy, and Sensitivity Training. Modal responses were typically "not at all" and "a small amount." However, 53% of institutions reported using small group seminars "extensively."

Cooperating school districts and cooperating teachers. Overall, 38% of institutions reported having written contracts with cooperating districts. The average distance student teachers traveled was 20 miles. Various methods were used to train cooperating teachers, including seminars (52%), workshops (33%), conferences (31%), a formal course (27%), and newsletters (27%). Major characteristics sought in cooperating teachers included willingness to have a student teacher (45%), and human relations skills.

Institutions of higher education reported being satisfied with the "competency" of cooperating teachers, with 44% indicating "very well" and 41% "quite well." The most common benefits offered to cooperating teachers included library privileges (46%), consulting services (28%), and "some free tuition" (25%). About 76% provided stipends to cooperating teachers, which averaged $58 ($443 in 2019 dollars). About 27% of institutions reported providing a graduate course in the supervision of student teachers, with 85% of cooperating teachers reported having taken such a course (Johnson, 1968).

EMERGING KNOWLEDGE BASE

From the late 1950s to the early 1980s, teacher education was seen as a "training problem," or a matter of how to teach behaviors that matched those of teachers seen as effective. From today's point of view, this approach appears to be rooted in a technical, behavioral view of teaching. The point of research was to determine how to teach how to apply these effective behaviors to classroom situations to produce student learning gains, or demonstrating the relationship between teacher behavior to student achievement. This type of research parallels the "minimal competency" movement of the 1970s and is referred to as "process-product research" (Arends, 2006). It led to competency-based teacher training programs that became widespread in the late 1960s and early 1970s. Unfortunately, subsequent research was unable to show that these types of programs produced better teachers than others (Cochran-Smith, 2004).

Further complicating efforts to make headway in quality teacher preparation was the concept of "wash out." Edelfelt and Raths (1998) summarize, "The powerful socialization of the workplace, documented by Lortie (1975) and Rosenholtz (1989) washes out training effects" (p. 20). This notion posited that teacher candidates become more liberal and progressive toward K-12 schooling during their training, with a marked shift toward conservative, traditional views during student teaching that persists as they move into the field (Zeichner & Tabachnick, 1981). For example, Hoy and Rees (1977) found that although secondary-level student teacher belief systems remained relatively constant before and after student teaching, student teachers became more bureaucratic and custodial in their orientation toward schooling. They concluded that schools must change and that the idealistic orientation toward schooling inculcated in teacher preparation is not useful because of what student teachers are learning in the field. In essence, "wash out" blames K-12 schools for inhibiting innovation. However, Zeichner and Tabachnick (1981) pointed out issues with this notion, identifying a failure to scrutinize university practices, including economic and political contexts of the university environment. They claimed that this type of study is just as or more important than the study of school culture and its influence on teachers.

From the late 1980s through the early 2000s, teacher education began to be seen as a "learning problem" rather than a "training problem," in that the goal was to develop skilled professionals with the knowledge, skills, and dispositions to be highly adept decision-makers. Thus, the function of research in teacher education was to build the knowledge base beyond teacher behaviors and into the realm of studying the complex knowledge and decision-making of skilled teachers. During this time frame, multiple approaches to research developed, including critical approaches that involved exploring learning to teach diverse learners. Critiques of teacher education during this area included perceptions of the field being "touchy feely," with emphasis on beliefs and attitudes instead of being focused on student learning and student outcomes (Cochran-Smith, 2004).

END-OF-CENTURY CRITIQUES

The 1968 report can be seen as a first nationwide glimpse of student teaching as a common practice in the U.S. institutions of higher education. The subsequent explosion in research in the field of teacher education helped to solidify national consensus that student teaching was the most powerful, nearly universal experience in teacher preparation. However, in 1990 Guyton and McIntyre identified some significant critiques for the institution of student teaching, during this time period, summarized the following:

1. Conferences typically involved just the cooperating teacher and student teacher, with the student teacher taking a passive role.
2. Conferences typically involved low levels of thinking, and content discussed did not incorporate the research base on teaching practices.
3. Instead of using seminars to facilitate reflective teaching, they tended to focus on immediate classroom demands. They appeared to be extensions of the conference in this respect, but farther removed from classroom experience.
4. Feedback provided appeared to be based on general impressions rather than teaching ability and mastery of important skills. Reliability and validity of evaluations were called into question, as bias was found to be common.
5. Low failure or dropout rates for student teaching were reported as a complex issue, about which little was known.

These critiques come on the tails of a highly publicized and influential 1986 report entitled *Tomorrow's Teachers*, a report of the Holmes Group, co-sponsored by the Carnegie Corporation, the U.S. Department of Education, and other foundations. This consortium of deans and influential officials in education from around the country urged the reimagining of teacher preparation, tying professional preparation closely to the work of schools. Their recommendations included creating standards for entry to the profession and deepening partnerships, particularly by using what we now term "clinical faculty" who work across K-2 and higher education. They discussed briefly the role of the cooperating teacher and university supervisor, explaining how they need to work together to guide novices in understanding how to make important decisions in teaching. They recommended encouraging student teachers to take risks and innovate in the classroom, lamenting that "the emphasis is upon imitation of and subservience to the supervising teacher, not upon investment, reflection, and solving novel problems" (p. 55).

In general, the dominant view at the time was that student teaching did not appear to be fulfilling its potential, through disconnected theory and practice, and few opportunities for the student teacher to engage with the knowledge based as a reflective practitioner. Quality of the student teaching experience was thought to be over-dependent upon specific classroom sites headed by over-extended teachers, and the college or university lacked influence in all aspects of student teaching, from the selection of cooperating teachers to the overall day-to-day experience. By and large, student teaching activities were not based on knowledge of effective teaching practice. In sum, student teaching "involved a narrow range of classroom activities over which [student teachers] had little control" (Guyton & McIntyre, 1990, p. 521). These critiques aligned well with the concern with "wash out" presented above.

To this end, some end-of-century work posited new directions for student teaching. For example, in 1987, Feiman-Nemser and Buchmann proposed a conceptual framework for student teaching that connected the research base in teaching to a new curriculum for student teaching, asking, "When is Student Teaching Teacher Education?" They discussed the need to develop complex ways of "pedagogical thinking and acting" (p. 257), concluding that "student teaching is teacher education when intending teachers are moved toward a practical understanding of the central tasks of teaching; when their dispositions and skills to extend and probe student learning are strengthened; when they learn to question what they see, believe, and do; when they see the limits of justifying their decisions and actions in terms of 'neat ideas' or classroom control; and when they see experience as a beginning rather than a culminating point in their learning" (p. 272).

Similarly, in 1991, Marilyn Cochran-Smith wrote about "Reinventing Student Teaching" buy building programs based on "collaborative resonance"—that is, connecting university-based theory with school-based practice through co-constructed learning communities. Again, deeper partnerships and breaking down traditional boundaries between K-12 and teacher preparation would be crucial to achieving this goal.

ASSESSMENT OF STUDENT TEACHING

"Standardizing the teacher preparation curriculum and the processes used to prepare teachers were . . . the means used for most of the 20th century to ensure that teachers were competent" (Arends, 2006, p. 6). Assessment of student teaching remained poor and came under attack as it proved impervious to efforts at standardization. Through the 1980s, evaluations were given primarily through final assessments conducted by cooperating teachers and field supervisors. Grades were then given to a course, weighted heavily by the assessment of the college supervisor. These evaluations were based on "a single overall affective impression rather than on distinct professional competencies" (Lucas, 1997, p. 526). Even when specific standards were used for student teacher performance, reliability and validity were questionable. Few failed student teaching, grades clustered at the upper end of the continuum and failed to distinguish between candidates. Further, few institutions of higher education had processes in place to prevent problems in student teaching or to intervene with student teachers who needed additional support (Lucas, 1997).

Efforts at standardization in assessing the outcomes of student teaching came through the licensure and certification process, which fell increasingly under state and federal control. In the 1980s and 1990s, several high profile national publications came together to shine a spotlight on the importance of high standards for teacher preparation, performance assessments for both pre-service and in-service teachers, and standardized licensure processes. These publications came on the heels of the now-famed A Nation At Risk, which spurred national concern about the perceived lack of progress of America's youth in education and led to a flurry of testing in both K-12 and teacher preparation (Arends, 2006). For example, the 1996 What Matters Most, Report of the National Commission on Teaching and America's Future, brought together work of the fledging National Board for Professional Teaching Standards and Interstate New Teacher Assessment and Support Consortium (INTASC) with NCATE to provide "a blueprint for recruiting, preparing, and supporting excellent teachers in all of America's Schools" (NCTAF, 1996, p. 10). Later, a remodeled teacher education accreditation process, now referred to as NCATE 2000, shifted national accreditation from a focus on process standards to a comprehensive assessment system to measure and report candidate performance (Arends, 2006).

By the 1990s, state policy around teacher education was common, particularly in the areas of teacher certification and licensure. The most common policy among states regarding preservice teacher education was to specify credit hour minimums for coursework in professional education or the number of courses in specific subjects, such as classroom management and subject-specific pedagogy (Lucas, 1997). By 2000, all states required a Bachelor's degree for licensure. Forty-two states required teacher testing, most to assess pedagogical and content knowledge, fourteen had Professional Standards Boards, and many had specific staged licensure processes (Wilson & Youngs, 2005).

With respect to student teaching, by the mid-1980s, student teaching was required by all states. Common regulations included specifying the structure and length of experiences, subject and/or grade level of student teaching assignments, criteria for selection of assignments in terms of district and school, and requirements for supervision and evaluation. Less common were criteria for selecting cooperating teachers. Policies on student teacher to supervisor ratios varied from 1-1 to 30-1 (Guyton & McIntyre, 1990).

State policy was also the subject of prominent discussion in the field. In a 2005 anthology on research in teacher education, Cochran-Smith and Fries promote studying teacher education as a policy problem, noting that previous studies had been inconsistent on whether teacher preparation and certification are central to teacher quality. They posited a great need for "uniform measures of 'impact' and 'effectiveness'" (p. 96) in order to provide evidence to guide the decisions of policymakers, accounting for the wide variety in school contexts that exists in the United States. This line of thinking became crucial later on during the wave of accountability that began at the beginning of the next century (Cochran-Smith, 2004).

In conclusion, fears of falling behind in education worldwide helped usher in a new wave of interest in reform in teacher education as a way to boost teacher quality. Highly visible critiques and recommendations for reform dominated the field. National studies and reports helped clarify current practices and needs, both practical and theoretical. An emerging knowledge base in teacher education helped guide practice and solidify the centrality of student teaching to quality teacher education. Shifting views of teaching and learning dominated both theory and practice in teacher education. Expanded state and even federal influence, as well as continued efforts by national organizations, expanded requirements and created even more uniformity in student teaching through standardizing assessment and teacher licensing processes.

Chapter 4

Current Context in Teacher Preparation

Arguably, one of the most significant themes in current research and practice in teacher preparation relates to various aspects of field experiences. Repeatedly, the research literature has tied quality fieldwork to later teacher effectiveness, emphasizing the centrality of school-university partnerships to those experiences. The growth in the use of performance assessments in teacher preparation also reflects the increased emphasis on authentic experiences. All of these pressures have led to a significant push toward a comprehensive redesign of teacher preparation programs. This transformation has begun to make its mark on the student teaching experience, as we explore in chapter 7.

Professional organizations in teacher education have taken a significant role in the call for increased quality and quantity of field experience. In fact, the latest wave of attention to field experiences can be traced back to the now widely cited 2010 National Council for the Accreditation of Teacher Education (NCATE) Blue Ribbon Panel, which provoked the higher education community by proposing that teacher preparation be "turned upside down," placing field experiences at the center of programs instead of traditional college coursework (NCATE, 2010). The creation of the Council for the Accreditation of Educator Preparation (CAEP) in 2013 resulted in significant changes in accreditation requirements. These changes mirrored the field's emphasis on the centrality of "clinical practice" in teacher preparation programs. Rust and Clift (2015) define clinical practice as a "high-powered instructional strategy that is designed to enable the learner to make connections between professional coursework and the interpersonal and context-bound setting of the actual workplace" (p. 48–49). In general, it is seen as enhanced field experiences in its attention to contextualized mentoring and seamless connection with coursework.

The new accreditation standards not only raised requirements for field experiences but also began requiring teacher preparation programs to provide outcome data on the effectiveness of these experiences, including impact on K-12 learners (CAEP, 2013). In 2015, the American Association of Colleges for Teacher Education (AACTE) convened its Clinical Practices Commission, with a charge of defining and describing clinical practices in teacher preparation. In 2018 this Commission unveiled a set of ten "Proclamations" designed to guide the development of clinical experiences in teacher preparation (AACTE, 2018a).

Despite these significant and seemingly focused changes to the profession, several issues continue to challenge the field. For example, large variations in practice both within and across institutions of higher education produce uneven quality in field experiences and hinder research in identifying evidence-based practices (Hollins, 2015). Declining enrollment in and financial support for traditional university-based programs also makes growth and development more challenging. Finally, accountability in teacher preparation remains elusive, despite increased accreditation requirements and state-level efforts attempting to tie teacher performance to preparation programs (Sindelar et al., 2014; Zeichner & Bier, 2018).

In sum, reform efforts directed toward boosting the quality and quantity of clinical practices in teacher preparation have succeeded in changing the discourse and least some practices in the field. Although many of the previous critiques of teacher preparation remain valid, efforts have been made by leaders in the field to address the research- to practice gap and to focus reform squarely on the creation of clinical practices in teacher preparation. As the single common culminating experience in the vast majority of teacher preparation programs, the student teaching experience is placed squarely in the spotlight of this significant shift in practice.

CURRENT CRITIQUES OF TEACHER PREPARATION

In 2006, there existed over 1,200 schools, colleges, and departments of teacher education located within 78% of all U.S. four-year colleges and universities (Levine, 2006). Newer data indicate that colleges and universities currently prepare about two-thirds of all teachers in the United States (Zeichner, 2018). Despite these impressive numbers, researchers agree that schools of education still have not attained the status or legitimacy afforded to many other academic areas. In fact, they "have been the subject of mounting criticism . . . from academics, think tanks, professional and scholarly associations, and government" (Levine, 2006, pp. 5–6). This low status within the university community is long-standing and well documented and has hindered progress in multiple ways over the past decade, even with the unfolding of a strong reform movement (Zeichner, 2018).

For example, education schools are dogged by charges of having the least selective admission standards, disorganized programs emphasizing theory over practice, insufficient mentoring, and hiring professionals who are disconnected from the field (Levine, 2006). Unfortunately, as the interest in clinical partnerships has risen, those involved in this critical work have failed to attain greater status within the system in which they were already marginalized. The individuals responsible for mentoring and assessing teacher candidates in the schools typically include adjunct faculty or doctoral students, often employed on a part-time and/or temporary basis and lacking even basic-decision-making power within the college or university. Those who do work across K-12 and higher education settings often find themselves lacking a home base, permanent position, and/or clear expectations for their roles. When full-time, tenure track faculty are engaged in this valuable work, the significant work that accompanies this role often goes unrewarded, as it falls outside the bounds of traditional teaching and research expectations. Further, the fix of hiring full-time "clinical faculty" to serve in these roles has fallen short of its promise as well (Zeichner & Bier, 2018).

One of the most significant and long-standing criticisms of teacher preparation is the disconnect between course- and fieldwork, or the research-to-practice gap. According to the Fordham Foundation's highly critical report, Cracks in the Ivory Tower, teacher educators focus on "idealism, good intensions, and progressivist thinking" over what school personnel considers the most challenging aspects of teaching, such as classroom management and implementing state standards (Farkas & Duffett, 2011, p. 8). This disconnect between what is learned in college coursework and what teacher candidates experience in school-based placements is so deep-rooted and the barriers between K-12 and higher education so significant that it is challenging to overcome, even when strong university/school partnerships are present.

Zeichner and Bier (2018) operationalize this issue by providing several common scenarios. For example, they describe teacher candidates being placed with cooperating or mentor teachers who have very little if any knowledge of the university program, and university faculty who have little if any knowledge of the cooperating or mentor teachers or their classrooms. Differing or competing philosophies and/or teaching methods across school and university are commonplace. Even when teacher candidates do receive mentoring to assist them in making sense of their coursework within the context of real-world practice, the mentors are often overextended, underpaid, and underprepared for the complex demands they are being asked to undertake. "As a result of this lack of a shared vision and common goals, the usual ways in which placements are determined and the structure of the cooperating/mentor teachers' roles, teacher candidates frequently do not have opportunities to observe, try out and receive detailed feedback on their teaching of the methods they learn about in their coursework" (Zeichner & Bier, 2015, p. 23).

Further, the knowledge base linking specific practices to outcomes in teacher preparation is quite limited. Although the field has general knowledge that both practical experiences and college courses do appear to have a positive impact on teacher candidate learning and teaching practice, little research has documented this impact in a manner that can be replicated or that extends longitudinally into teachers' later practice. Much of the existing research relies on small, contextual samples and is documented in the form of data from a single partnership or institution of higher education. Although strong school-university partnerships can reduce the theory-to-practice gap, this impact is not always measurable and/or linked to future changes in practice. In sum, "Learning to practice is impacted by individual, instructional, and contextual factors—some of which we are only beginning to understand" (Clift & Brady, 2006, p. 331). Efforts to link teacher quality back to preparation programs through Value Added Modeling (VAM) or other statewide assessment practices have also been unsuccessful (Sindelar et al., 2014). The inconclusive results of these larger investigations have spawned further criticism nationally, leading some influential individuals and groups to conclude that traditional college- and university-based teacher preparation programs should be dismantled and replaced by various alternatives (Imig et al., 2014; Sindelar et al., 2014).

CURRENT TRENDS IN RESEARCH AND PRACTICE

The growth of what is now labeled "alternative routes to licensure" stems from the 1980s, which saw the emergence of the first non-college- and university-based teacher preparation programs. Generally, these programs offer fast-track, flexible licensure paths that bypass many of the typical undergraduate requirements, targeting career-changers who already possess college degrees. The concept behind these routes was that they would bring new individuals into the teaching profession, such as people of color, men, and former military personnel, and that these individuals would be more committed to the profession than those on emergency contracts (Zeichner, 2018).

Another milestone in the growth of alternative, or "nontraditional" routes to licensure can be traced to the No Child Left Behind Act of 2001, which supported the need "to establish, expand or enhance a teacher recruitment and retention program for high-quality mid-career professionals . . . and recent graduates of an institution of higher education" (NCLB, 2001, p. 1657).

Supporters also believed this provision would bring new and talented individuals into the profession, while opponents claimed that it simply lowered the bar to the profession and devalued the extensive training provided to other novice teachers (Sindelar et al., 2014). In 2004, a highly publicized address given by the then-superintendent of Boston Public Schools offered a significant criticism of college- and university-based programs for failing to prepare effective teachers who remained in the profession. Later, this individual developed one of the first "Teacher Residency" programs, designed after preparation for the medical field and aimed at preparing teachers for and within specific districts, using a variety of university and other community partners (Zeichner, 2018).

Despite their vast differences, much controversy remains over these "nontraditional" programs, which have most recently been redefined as those providing individuals with the opportunity to gain teacher certification in a structured program while concurrently teaching in a classroom with support and supervision (Haj-Broussard et al., 2015). Some of these routes are characterized by only a few weeks of dedicated training or require candidates simply to pass exams. Many nontraditional programs are run by public or charter schools or operate as independent graduate schools. Some have predicted that their growth will render traditional college- and university-based teacher preparation programs obsolete, despite the fact that colleges and universities continue to prepare the vast majority of this nation's teachers (Zeichner, 2018).

Over the past ten to fifteen years, significant research has attempted to compare outcomes or effectiveness of various types of teacher preparation programs. However, due to the wide variety of these programs and the blurring of the lines between "traditional" and "nontraditional" or "alternative," research has not been able to demonstrate the superiority of one preparation model over another. Nevertheless, concerns and critiques continue on both sides of this issue (Sindelar et al., 2014). With respect to student teaching, alternative routes to licensure are significant because they involve extensive preparation in the field with intensive coaching, privileging fieldwork over coursework. Their structures often follow other research-based practices at least in theory, including closer alignment between course- and fieldwork, bridging preservice training and induction supports, and often employing individuals as fully fledged teachers in the same building or district in which they completed their student teaching or internship.

All of these critiques of "traditional" college- and university-based teacher preparation have simply intensified the call for reform outlined previously. Below we discuss the foundations of this movement, beginning with theory and practice, and continuing with responsibilities of professional organizations. We conclude with a summary of present challenges, leading into direct impact of the student teaching experience.

The general importance of fieldwork, or immersing teacher candidates in practices in the schools, has been investigated and agreed upon for decades, finding its way into every published anthology in teacher preparation (e.g., Buttery et al., 1996; Cochran-Smith & Zeichner, 2005; Houston et al., 1990). Research has shown repeatedly that novice teachers consider field experience to be the most critical aspect of their preparation programs, and researchers in the field have called continuously for both increased quality and quantity of those experiences (NCATE, 2010). Further, teacher educators appear to agree with the general principle that practical placements are critical to teacher development and should combine carefully guided developmental experiences and intensive supports (Hoffman et al., 2005).

As a case in point, the long-standing and widespread Professional Development Schools (PDS) model demonstrates an early commitment to enhancing and deepening field experiences and connecting those experiences to more traditional university coursework (Cochran-Smith & Zeichner, 2005). Originally dating to the work of the Holmes Group in the 1980s, this model is supported by the work of the National Network for Educational Renewal (NNER) and embodied in the National Association for Professional Development Schools (NAPDS). The National Council for the Accreditation of Teacher Preparation defines this particular type of partnership as "innovative institutions formed through partnerships between professional development educational programs and P-12 schools. Their mission is professional preparation of candidates, faculty development, inquiry directed at the improvement of practice, and enhanced student learning" (NCATE, 2001, p. 1). This movement also maintains a stated commitment to innovation and social justice (Brenault & Lack, 2009; Zenkov et al., 2013).

As this structure grew in popularity, so too did the diversity of partnerships calling themselves PDS models. The 1990s saw the development of multiple sets of standards intended to define and guide the movement (Breault & Lack, 2009). Thousands of research studies have targeted this model, but like other models in teacher education, much of the research has focused on single partnerships and perceptions, with little attention given to outcomes (Breault & Breault, 2012). Many existing studies tout the benefits of the PDS model, including comparing quality of PDS field placements favorably to quality of non-PDS field placements, pointing to tighter connections between course- and fieldwork, and the assistance with teacher induction and retention (Zenkov et al., 2013). However, critics claim that existing models have not lived up to their potential or rhetoric, particularly in the area of innovation and social justice. In other words, "The PDS model, as it is presently conceived, is simply not up to the task of bringing about true educational equity and may not even be the best road to equal achievement" (Breault & Lack, 2009, p. 165).

More recently, efforts have been directed toward other models that expand and tighten traditional field experience in teacher preparation. In fact, the term "clinical experience" has all but replaced the term "field experience" in the professional literature. This shift connotes the need to place practical experiences at the center of teacher education rather than at the periphery, intensifying them, and increasing intentional connections to coursework through strong K-12 partnerships (Maheady et al., 2004). Others have delineated critical aspects of partnerships, such as using clinical faculty (employed by K-12 schools, universities, or a combination of both) to deliver intensive coaching and realigning expectations with coursework, often created and delivered jointly by K-12 and university partners (Hollins, 2015). Coaching and mentoring is considered a critical part of innovation in teacher preparation overall (Hoffman et al., 2015). Zeichner (2010) coined the concept of "third space" in teacher preparation, which he defined as "hybrid spaces in preservice teacher education programs that bring together school and university-based teacher educators and practitioner and academic knowledge in new ways to enhance the learning of prospective teachers" (p. 92). This term has assisted in defining critical aspects of clinical preparation in the effort to reform and restructure the field.

As attention has centered on reforming clinical experiences, creating increased attention to measuring teacher candidate performance in the field. Historically, student teachers were graded simply by cooperating teachers and field supervisors, and for the past thirty years, states have also required various pencil-and-paper (or computer-based) assessments in content and pedagogy (Wilson & Youngs, 2005). However, the shift to performance standards in K-12 education in the late 1990s and early 2000s soon precipitated a similar shift in teacher preparation.

The goal of performance assessment of teaching is to present data on individual candidate performance as well as to provide program faculty and administrators with strengths and needs to guide program redesign (Stillman et al., 2015). In 1998, California passed legislation requiring successful completion of a performance assessment in order to earn an initial teaching credential. These assessments were described as "subject-specific portfolios of teaching with a standardized set of integrated tasks that ask teachers to document their planning, teaching, assessing, and reflecting around a series of lessons on a topic of their own choice" (Chung, 2008, p. 8) Now common, these performance assessments were grounded in (1) 1980s research on the "reflective practitioner"; and (2) 1990s research on K-12 performance assessments to evaluate student learning and encourage higher-order thinking (Chung, 2008).

Currently, the most utilized preservice teacher performance assessment is the edTPA, created and developed over time by Stanford University. Dozens of versions of this assessment have been validated and implemented across the United States to encompass subject-specific pedagogy for various licensure fields, but they are all structured around the planning, implementation, and evaluation teaching cycle. The assessment involves "using authentic artifacts of teaching practice, analytic rubrics measuring teaching behaviors associated with student learning and an integrative, multiple-measures assessment of teaching" (Stillman et al., 2015, p. 181). These assessments now serve as high-states exams in dozens of states, as individuals are required to receive a certain score in order to receive their teaching licenses (Blanton et al., 2014).

In sum, all of these critiques of practice and reform efforts have converged in the professional literature in a repeated call to redesign traditional college and university preparation programs in their entirety. This call has been echoed consistently in major reviews of the literature (e.g., Hollins, 2015) and reports of professional organizations. These national organizations have begun the work of further defining, organizing, and providing examples of the kinds of structures and roles that typify "clinical practice" in teacher preparation.

RESPONSES OF PROFESSIONAL ORGANIZATIONS

In 2010, the then-largest accrediting body in teacher preparation (National Council on Accreditation of Teacher Education, NCATE) published a now-renowned manifesto urging an intensive and immediate shift toward clinically based teacher preparation. This often-cited "Blue Ribbon Panel Report" proposed turning "teacher preparation upside down and revamping programs to place clinical practice at the center of teacher preparation" (as quoted in Imig et al., 2011, p. 404).

That same year, the largest professional organization in teacher education, AACTE, published a Policy Brief entitled, "The Clinical Preparation of Teachers." This brief identified six "Critical Components of Clinical Preparation," including strong partnerships, the use of clinical educators, and jointly designed teacher education curricula and supports. It also provided examples of high-quality clinical preparation and made recommendations to guide federal policy and teacher preparation providers (AACTE, 2010).

Also, about this time, the two major professional accrediting bodies in teacher preparation, NCATE and TEAC (Teacher Education Accreditation Council), merged into a new accrediting body, CAEP. This reorganization reflected the push toward clinical preparation in its newly designed standards. Two standards addressed this change directly, Standard 2, Clinical Partnership and Practice, and Standard 4, Program Impact. Standard 2 required educator preparation programs to demonstrate evidence of mutually beneficial partnerships, the preparation and use of high-quality clinical educators, and the impact of the variety of clinical experience and assessment. Assessments must be designed to demonstrate candidates' effectiveness and positive impact on P-12 student learning and growth. Standard 4 required programs to document growth in teacher candidates in multiple ways, including P-12 impact measures (CAEP, 2013). These changes in requirements for teacher preparation programs seeking professional accreditation marked a significant shift for teacher preparation on a national scale (Imig et al., 2011).

Also, about the same time, the Council of Chief State School Officers (CCSSO) published another related report entitled, "Our Responsibility, Our Promise: Transforming Educator Preparation and Entry into the Profession." This report reiterated many of the challenges of teacher preparation presented in this chapter, including the wide variation in policy and practice. The authors made four recommendations for reform in teacher preparation, including increased selectivity for program entry and exit, aligning teacher supply with demand, enhancing preparation for the use of assessment in instruction, and clinically based approaches to preparation. The report highlighted the quality of clinical experiences and the important and diverse roles of clinical educators in enhanced preparation (CCSSO, 2010).

One of the most recent developments in the unfolding of change in teacher preparation involves AACTE's continuing work in clinical practice. In 2015, AACTE convened the Clinical Practice Commission in order to "further operationalize the recommendations of the NCATE Blue Ribbon Panel Report" (AACTE, 2018, p. 1). The authors claimed that although the Blue Ribbon Panel spawned new interest in and a significant wave of school-based partnerships, the varied practices that formed led to "divergent understanding of terms, structure, and quality." The Commission then presented ten "Essential Proclamations and Tenets for Highly Effective Clinical Educator Preparation," including definitions of clinical practice, clinical educators, and partnerships. The tenets emphasized the developmental nature of teacher preparation, the collaborative nature of partnership through the inclusion of all stakeholders, the importance of a strong partnership infrastructure, and attention to high-leverage practices throughout the design process. Follow-up activities include the creation of an additional task force dedicated to applying the framework to the field of special education, as well as clinical preparation videos to guide practice and numerous research-to-practice sessions at national conferences (aacte.org).

In sum, current directions in teacher preparation appear to have aligned significantly since the 2010 Blue Ribbon Panel Report. As interest in clinical preparation has grown, national professional organizations have attempted to define principles and parameters for clinical preparation that are in concert with current research and best practices. However, despite the single-minded focus on redesigning teacher education around clinical preparation principles, multiple issues continue to challenge the field.

Continuing Challenges

The significant shift in rhetoric in teacher preparation over the past two decades appears to have spurred some changes in the field, particularly with respect to enhanced K-12/higher education partnerships and attention to clinical experiences. However, as AACTE's Clinical Practice Commission points out, these efforts have led to significant variation in practices, to the extent that the Committee felt a need to define and delimit what constitutes "clinical practices" in the field (AACTE, 2018b). Further, significant gaps in the existing research continue to plague the field. Sindelar et al. (2014) explain that in today's political climate, "Student achievement gain has become the gold standard with which teacher preparation is judged" (p. 4). Because few, if any, links have been discovered between teacher preparation and student achievement as discussed earlier, some have concluded that teacher preparation has no impact on teacher quality. This conclusion has further weakened the support of many influential individuals and national groups with respect to the value of traditional college and university preparation programs (Sindelar et al., 2014).

Another challenge of the past decade has been a significant decrease in enrollment in teacher preparation programs nationally, despite an increase in the number of Bachelor's degrees granted overall. A recent AACTE report noted a 23% decline in the completion of teacher preparation programs between 2008 and 2016. According to the report, the most significant reason for this trend is a drop in the public's perception of the desirability of a teaching career, pointing to low wages and a lack of professional autonomy. This climate of lowered interest in entering the teaching profession certainly presents an additional challenge to colleges and universities attempting to reinvent themselves.

Concomitant with the lowered funding due to enrollment decreases is a decrease in funding targeting teacher preparation targeting teacher preparation from the federal government and philanthropic community. Federal policies over the past fifteen years have "encouraged states to deregulate teacher education and to open investment opportunities to non-university providers" (Zeichner, 2018, p. 7), as well as led to actions on the part of education philanthropists to fund alternative providers. Zeichner (2018) argues that both of these funding streams have worked to "disrupt" the current college- and university-based system, as well as spurred an increase in the creation of non-college and university-based providers of teacher preparation, both nonprofits and for-profits. As Sindelar et al. (2014) summarize, "After decades of unquestioned authority over who enters the profession, we have lost the confidence and support of policy makers and the public alike. We now endeavor to demonstrate that what we do makes a difference, particularly on outcomes of importance. Meanwhile, alternatives to traditional teacher preparation proliferate, and the questions about preparation have become how little is required and how quickly can it get done?" (p. 7).

The persistent attempt by researchers to tie teacher preparation to later P-12 student outcomes has also impacted the field. Although valuable, this type of research represents a global look at preparation rather than a nuanced one that considers various programmatic elements such as coursework and specific structures related to field experiences. Further, attempting to establish these links mirrors larger methodological issues, such as the challenges involved in measuring teacher effectiveness in a valid and reliable way, and controlling for the myriad variables contributing to the knowledge held and skills employed by novice teachers. However, these lines of research are likely to flourish in today's results-oriented political climate despite the drawbacks mentioned. Needed in further research are "well-designed smaller-scale studies that have the capacity to examine closely the content and practice of teaching and the link to student achievement as well as studies drawing on large-scale databases to show what components of a teacher's preparation contribute to student learning and behavior" (Blanton et al., 2014, p. 140).

In conclusion, the current context in the field of teacher preparation as a profession is challenging for researchers and practitioners alike. Decades of critiques of traditional college- and university-based preparation have led to focused calls for a specific reform agenda grounded in "clinical practice" from both inside and outside the profession. These themes are illustrated in research, practice, and highly publicized reports from national organizations. However, critiques have also led to competition in teacher preparation in the form of "alternative" or "nontraditional" programs. Additional issues include significant variation in practices, the struggle to establish a link between preparation and novice teacher quality, declining enrollment in teacher preparation programs, and lack of conclusive research linking specific program structures to later teacher quality. The following chapter places a spotlight on current practices in student teaching and presents the research that has been conducted on this common experience, as one that could provide the field with guidance needed to lead reform efforts in teacher preparation.

Chapter 5

Current Context in Student Teaching

Over the past century and a half, "student teaching has moved from limited experiences in laboratory schools to full-time, multiweek assignments in real settings (public schools)" (Edelfelt & Raths, 1998, p. 19). By the 1950s, accreditation had begun assessing conditions and processes surrounding student teaching and other elements of preparation, and by 2000, attention had turned to the products and outcomes of various structures in teacher education, including student teaching (Edelfelt & Raths, 1998; Cochran-Smith, 2004).

Despite controversy over methodology, several issues have had significant impact on the quality of research in student teaching in the shift to a focus on outcomes (Boyd et al., 2009; National Council on Teacher Quality, 2012). These issues include how to remove the influence of self-selection into teacher preparation programs, the knowledge that programs place student teachers into different settings for varied reasons, the factors contributing to teacher placement into their first teaching positions, and myriad other variables that need to be controlled in order to make conclusive statements about the impact of student teaching. The "gold standard" in this body of research involves tying student teaching to later teacher quality.

In 2011, the National Council on Teacher Quality (NCTQ) engaged in a critical review of the research literature on student teaching. The report reviewed articles published in dozens of leading journals in teacher education between 1997 and 2011. The authors identified thirty-four studies that met their quality indicators. They grouped these studies into four categories: student teaching programs in general, nature of the relationship between preparation programs and partner schools, student teachers' perceptions of their experiences, and supervision of student teachers. Only three of the thirty-four studies attempted to link aspects of student teaching with future teacher effectiveness, and only one did not employ a case study approach. The vast majority of the studies identified in the interview focused on the partnership between preparation programs and K-12 schools, and the nature of the supervisory experience (Greenberg et al., 2011).

CONTEMPORARY RESEARCH ON PARTNERSHIPS AND SUPERVISION

In 2002, a special section of Teacher Education Quarterly was devoted to student teaching. Zeichner (2002) summarizes the findings of this collection of manuscripts in five primary points: (1) the student teaching experience is critical to quality teacher preparation, with cooperating teachers as key players; (2) cooperating teachers must be both good teachers and effective mentors; (3) learning to be an effective mentor is a challenging and complex process; (4) attention to ensuring a supportive environment and positive relationships is crucial for positive outcomes in student teaching; and (5) a close match between practices utilized in the student teaching placement and those advocated in the remainder of the teacher preparation program is crucial. Zeichner identified common barriers to following these principles, including the relatively low status of the work of mentoring student teachers in both K-12 and higher education settings, and the common yet significant disconnect between campus-based components of teacher education and the student teaching experience itself.

Zeichner concluded his summary by recommending comprehensive partnership as a way to "break out of the box of the traditional student teaching model" (2002, p. 62). These partnerships should include several crucial elements: viewing the school and community as the placement site, rather than a single classroom; planning for broader learning regarding community and culture; increased use of site-based (pre-student teaching) courses and supervisors; utilizing school staff to design and implement teacher education curricula; and raising the status of clinical supervision in both K-12 and higher education settings.

More recent research on student teaching has supported the conclusions of this summary. For example, Johnson and Napper-Owen (2011) examined role perceptions in the student teaching triad, which refers to student teachers, cooperating teachers, and university supervisors. Their analysis showed the importance of particular role perceptions of student teaching success. In particular, they identified a need for greater clarity in role definition and enhanced communication among the individuals involved in the student teaching process. Cherian (2007) reinforced the importance of various aspects of cooperating teachers' support to preservice teachers' development, particularly opportunities for reflection. However, the author also cautioned that some mentors' beliefs and pressures can hinder this development.

Steadman and Brown (2011) identified a significant gap in the research on university supervisors, who are often part-time faculty or graduate students with limited access to and knowledge of the teacher preparation program. They examined the beliefs and practices of members of one teacher education department, finding that although university faculty felt supervision was important, it was not provided much time or attention by the group when compared to other program practices. These faculty did not provide training to their doctoral student supervisors even though they perceived such training as necessary. Further, supervisory practices varied widely within the one institution, in terms of number of visits, conferencing, and even in completing required forms related to the supervision. Ways of interacting with student teachers, role perceptions, and focus of the visits varied widely as well. For example, St. John et al. (2018) documented the complex process of assigning student teachers to cooperating teachers. Despite each party's interest in making good matches, the process was difficult to follow, complicated by individuals' perceptions of what makes a good cooperating teacher and a good match, and by the partnership itself.

All of the issues appear to have a significant impact on student teachers. Fives et al. (2007) examined early signs of burnout among teacher candidates at two different times during their student teaching experience. The relationship between burnout and efficacy was quite strong. Those student teachers reporting more guidance from their cooperating teachers and more support from their university supervisors reported higher levels of efficacy than those who reported less guidance and support. Although causality could not be established due to the methodology utilized in this study, the authors suggested increasing opportunities to enhance efficacy during the student teaching experience. They posit that attention to these issues during student teaching might serve as a mediator for the drop in efficacy that typically occurs during the first year of teaching.

An ecological study conducted by Valencia et al. (2009) on triad interactions helps place these studies in context. They summarized previous literature by stating, "The dynamics [of the triad are] complicated and challenging, resulting in disappointing professional development for preservice teachers" (p. 305). They completed a four-year longitudinal study of novice language arts teachers, beginning with their student teaching experience and following them into their first three years of teaching.

The authors summarized their findings by referring to the student teaching experience as a "lost opportunity for learning to teach" (p. 318). Although each member of the triad acted on how they understood their role, the process was hindered by tensions surrounding differing views of effective teaching and learning, and the overall goals of the student teaching experience. The authors found limited opportunities to give and receive feedback, share valuable knowledge among the triad. They also reported a lack of support for mentoring and unclear criteria for expectations throughout the experience. The need to maintain harmony among the actors often stood at odds with the need for critical conversations and feedback that could contribute to the student teacher's growth. The authors speculated that this climate might be the cause of previous research findings indicating the "limited influence of cooperating teachers and university supervisors on student teacher learning" (p. 319).

Interestingly, seven years later, Burns et al. (2016) found the role of university supervisor to be changing in light of the push to enhance and deepen clinical experiences. Using qualitative meta-analysis techniques, the authors reviewed the professional literature in the area of student teaching supervision from 2001 to 2013. They found thirty-two articles that met their criteria for topic and robustness of analysis.

The authors made the important distinction between "evaluation" and "supervision" in their analysis, in considering the supportive and educative role of the university supervisor. They asserted the need to see beyond the role of "targeted assistance," the cycle of observation and feedback that is most often ascribed to university supervisors. They posited that the broadened tasks they uncovered were related to the push for richer clinical experiences. These five tasks include the following:

1. Targeted Assistance: providing focused instructional feedback and fostering critical reflection
2. Individual Support: providing both challenge and support within the student teaching experience and helping teacher candidates cope with stress
3. Collaboration and Community: developing quality placements, maintaining triad relationships, and creating learner-centered communities for and with teacher candidates
4. Curriculum Support: fostering connections between theory and practice and strengthening curriculum planning for teacher preparation
5. Research for Innovation: engaging in inquiry for self-study, and innovating to enhance supervision

Finally, the authors identify "shared supervisory roles" that are taking shape as higher education—K12 partnerships deepen. These roles are filled by individuals in positions titled liaison, clinical faculty or clinical educator, and professional development associate (Burns et al., 2016).

TYING STUDENT TEACHING TO
TEACHER EFFECTIVENESS

The single study identified by Greenberg et al. (2011) that met all of their quality indicators was an evaluation of the preparation programs supplying first-year teachers to New York City Schools. This study attempted to examine the relationship between these programs and later K-12 outcomes. Published in 2009 by Boyd, Grossman, Lankford, Loeb, and Wyckoff, the study found that the program from which candidates graduated was in fact related to later teaching effectiveness. Although not directly and specifically related to the student teaching experience, the authors examined programmatic aspects identified in the professional literature as most likely to impact program quality. These elements included "whether or not the program requires a capstone project, which is often a portfolio of work done in classrooms with students; the extent to which the program oversees the field experiences of its students; content knowledge requirements as measured by content courses in math and ELA, and the percentage of tenure-line faculty, a potential proxy for program stability and the extent to which institutions value teacher preparation" (p. 430). The authors then attempted to control for program self-selection and the variation between schools in which teachers were working through the use of three different analyses.

Results indicated that preparation program did appear to be related to teacher effectiveness, with effectiveness in teaching math and reading highly correlated. Some programs did change over time in terms of effectiveness. One specific aspect of teacher preparation seemed to make a difference in teacher quality, "teacher preparation that focuses more on the work of the classroom and provides opportunities for teachers to study what they will be doing" (p. 434). Although this finding appears self-evident, previous attempts to link any aspects of teacher preparation programs with future teacher quality had failed. Further, the authors identified specific practices that appeared to produce more effective teachers. These practices included more oversight of the student teaching experience, requiring a capstone project, and the specific study of curricula in context. These findings are significant in that they bolster the recommendations of researchers around the importance of providing carefully planned and supervised experiences that are grounded in practice and connected with coursework (e.g., Hollins, 2015; Zeichner, 2002).

NCTQ STUDY RESULTS

Based on the outcomes of their review, Greenberg et al. (2011) conducted a nationwide study that identified common characteristics of student teaching practices and then compared these practices against their findings. This research project took a stratified random sample of 134 institutions of higher education offering undergraduate elementary education programs, representing approximately 10% of the nation's traditional undergraduate programs in this area. Data included in the analysis included documents from institutions of higher education and partner districts, surveys of principals from partner districts, information collected from site visits, and policy that might impact the work of institutions of higher education in each state. They then compared practices at each of these institutions against five basic standards, condensed from an original nineteen developed from their literature review. These standards addressed intensity of the student teaching experience and important characteristics of the cooperating teacher.

The results of this study represent a crucial picture of the conditions of student teaching on a national level. First, in the area of teacher supply, the authors found 186,000 teachers graduating annually from teacher preparation programs, but only 77,000 actually taking a position in teaching. Second, with respect to the basic structure of student teaching, 99% of the institutions surveyed required full-time student teaching, with 91% prohibiting additional coursework. All required at least ten weeks of student teaching, with 75% sharing all of their cooperating teachers' responsibilities. Sixty-eight percent required student teachers to be present on the first day of school, and 75% required the experience to take place geographically close to the institution of higher education, as opposed to in distant urban areas or abroad.

Third, requirements for the selection of cooperating teachers varied. Most institutions of higher education (82%) required cooperating teachers to have a minimum number of years of experience teaching, primarily three. Twenty-eight percent reported using "effectiveness criteria" to select cooperating teachers, and 38% specified criteria of a good mentor. However, more than half (54%) of principals surveyed indicated their higher education partner did not specify any criteria for measuring or identifying cooperating teacher quality, and a similar number (52%) reported having no role in the selection of cooperating teachers. Finally, the study addressed the supervision of student teachers. Nearly half of the sample (48%) required five supervisory visits, and 43% provided criteria for assessment of supervisors, indicating they needed to demonstrate characteristics of effective teaching and effective mentoring.

The NCTQ study then compared this evidence to their standards, presenting recommendations based on this analysis. One recommendation was to produce fewer elementary teachers by raising standards for both student teachers and cooperating teachers. They recommended shrinking the pipeline by raising standards for entry into student teaching and by only recommending stronger candidates for licensure. The authors identified a significant shortage of cooperating teachers who met their standards, indicating a need for 40,000 additional "qualified" cooperating teachers annually. Their standards included at least three years of experience, measured effectiveness above the seventy-fifth percentile, demonstrated mentoring ability, and willingness to become a cooperating teacher.

Their second recommendation was to increase incentives for cooperating teachers, thus making mentoring more attractive to qualified candidates. Typically, the study found stipends to be very small, averaging about $250, which the authors claim does not begin to compensate teachers for their efforts. The authors recommended a deliberate attempt to increase prestige of their role, in addition to diverting more funds and other resources into supervision of student teaching.

In conclusion, the NCTQ study found student teaching to have sufficient quantity overall but lacking in quality. They reported that institutions of higher education have a lack of control over the student teaching process because of shortages of cooperating teachers, and districts determining which teachers serve as cooperating teachers. They recommend holding both teacher candidates and cooperating teachers to higher standards.

RECENT OUTCOME STUDIES

Recently, several researchers have taken on the significant challenge of attempting to tie student teaching experiences to later teacher effectiveness, as determined by K-12 student outcomes. Goldhaber et al. (2017) identified six such studies published between 2012 and 2015, summarizing that "while there is some variation across studies in how much of teacher effectiveness can be attributed to teacher education programs, these studies show that the vast majority of the variation in teacher effectiveness is within rather than between teacher education programs" (p. 327). They noted that "Harris and Sass (2011) consider several aspects of teacher education (e.g., the number of courses required in different areas), but find practically no evidence of a relationship between these observable aspects of teacher education and future teacher effectiveness" (p. 328). The authors reiterated the common challenges of being unable to control for differences in program selection and enrollment, as well as eventual employment in specific classrooms and schools (Goldhaber et al., 2017). The influence of each of these variables on later teacher effectiveness must be considered due to its potential for significant influence (e.g., Chetty et al., 2014; Kreig et al., 2016).

However, the work of Ronfeldt and colleagues has made progress in this area. They found that both teacher effectiveness and retention were related to having student taught in what they identified as "high-functioning schools" with lower turnover, even if candidates later took a position in a school with higher turnover (Ronfeldt, 2012). A subsequent study found the level of teacher collaboration in schools where teachers student taught to be predictive of later efficacy. Interestingly, this investigation also found that schools with a positive climate, as measured by collaboration, achievement gains, and less turnover, were less likely to be utilized as sites for field placement overall (Ronfeldt, 2015).

Using observational instead of value-added data as a marker of teacher effectiveness, a third study correlated effectiveness to various features of teacher preparation, including facets of the student teaching experience (Ronfeldt et al., 2018). This study found that teacher candidates who were hired into the school districts in which the students taught were significantly more effective than their peers. It also upheld the common view that more effective cooperating teachers tend to produce student teachers who are more effective in their first years of practice, although the measure was correlational. The authors found perceptions of preparedness taken at the end of student teaching to be unrelated to teacher effectiveness, suggesting that studies relying on these perceptions should be interpreted with caution. Further, novice teachers "i) received lower first-year observational ratings when they learned to teach in field placements with better average achievement and (ii) received no higher or lower first-year observational ratings based on their perceptions of the [field placements] having better working conditions. Field placement school level, socioeconomic status, and racial composition were not significantly associated with first-year teaching effectiveness" (p. 19). The authors concluded that there may not be drawbacks to placing student teachers in schools with lower test scores, but that positive school climate and stability of the teaching force in those schools do appear to matter. In sum, Goldhaber et al. (2017) reinforce the importance of the setting of student teaching to student teacher development as well as to later teacher effectiveness.

Two additional outcome studies showed that cooperating teachers who were effective with K-12 students based on value-added measures also appeared to produce better teachers, although the effect did lose strength after the first year of teaching (Goldhaber et al., 2018). One study explored the "match of place" between student teaching assignment and later school employment assignment, controlling for multiple variables that introduced bias in previous studies through the use of multiple analyses. They analyzed data from over twenty years of graduates from selected educator preparation programs in Washington, and from value-added data provided by the State of Washington.

In contrast to previous research that did not employ those controls, the authors found differences between educator preparation programs to be less significant than those within the same program, indicating the importance of studying within-institution variation. They did not find the characteristics of the student teaching school to predict later effectiveness, although those who taught in schools with higher percentages of students from underrepresented minority and low-income backgrounds were more effective in comparison to other teachers at the same school. Additionally, results showed this "match" between student teaching placement and later teaching assignment to be significant, in that a match is associated with higher student achievement and a mismatch with lower achievement. This finding was particularly significant for teachers working in what they identified as a "considerably more disadvantaged school than where they student taught" (p. 347) and was even more pronounced for schools with higher percentages of underrepresented minorities. The authors did not find any relationship between stronger candidate qualifications (e.g., test scores) and degree of match between student teaching placement and later school placement as a teacher.

Based on these findings, the authors recommended that (1) schools consider hiring their own student teachers; (2) educator preparation programs attempt to align candidate preferences with placement; and (3) educator preparation programs place teacher candidates they believe will be successful in schools with a greater concentration of students from disadvantaged backgrounds. They also urged more research tying specific experiences in teacher education more broadly, and in student teaching more specifically, with later teacher effectiveness in order to inform the field of teacher education.

Chapter 6

Comparison to Past Practice

Chapter 3 presents results of a 1968 nationwide survey on student teaching programs and practices, including information about program administration, supervision, cooperating teachers, and the student teachers themselves. This survey was the first of its kind in terms of scope and attention to detail surrounding the institution of student teaching. Chapter 5 summarizes the results of another nationwide study on the same topic, conducted forty-three years later, in 2011. Both studies surveyed the national landscape of student teaching in terms of common structures and practices. Although different survey instruments and sampling methods were used, formal and informal comparisons of those two studies reveal several important themes in the evolution of student teaching. In particular, comparisons reveal a standardization of practices, a loosening of K-12/university connections, and a shift in desired characteristics in cooperating teachers.

Further, the 1968 study presents qualitative data on what institutions of higher education believed constituted "innovations" in student teaching (Johnson, 1968). A contemporary analysis of this data reveals some "innovations" that are now commonplace, some that are obsolete, and others that are still considered innovations fifty years later. Other practices quantified in the 1968 study are also worth noting for the lack of later comparison data. Consideration of these practices of these practices provides a broader context from which to view current practice and future directions in student teaching.

STANDARDIZATION OF PRACTICES

The average length of the student teaching experience in the 1968 study was twelve weeks, with 79% of the sample requiring at least ten weeks. Further, 60% of secondary placements and 65% of elementary placements required full-time student teaching. In comparison, all of the institutions included in the second sample (2011) required at least ten weeks of student teaching. Further, in the second sample, 99% required full-time student teaching, with 91% prohibiting outside coursework. These findings indicate that minimum requirements have increased in the past forty years, with less variation.

In interpreting this comparison, the student teaching experience itself appears to be more consistent across the United States, in that it is now almost universally full-time and at least ten weeks in length. Certainly, the increase in uniformity is expected, given the increased influence of state policy, national organizations, and accreditors in the teacher education field (e.g., AACTE, 2010; CAEP, 2013). Another structure addressed in a more indirect manner in this study that appears to have remained virtually unchanged is that of the "student teaching triad" mentioned in the previous chapter. The 1968 study refers to the roles of student teacher, cooperating teacher, and supervisor, identical to roles as discussed in the 2011 study. Thus, the basic elements of student teaching appear to be unchanged in the past half-century.

LOOSENING OF K-12/UNIVERSITY CONNECTIONS

A general loosening of K-12/university connections can be seen through a variety of comparisons that can be made between the two studies. These comparisons include the number of supervisor visits, payment made to cooperating teachers, and training provided to cooperating teachers. Where direct data comparisons between the two studies could not be made due to differences in methodology, inferences were made by consulting the current professional literature.

With respect to the number of required visits on the part of the university supervisor, the 2011 study looked for a minimum of five supervisor visits, which translates to approximately one visit every two weeks. This study found that 48% of institutions held supervisors to this standard. In the initial sample, 72% had held supervisors to this standard, with 45% of institutions requiring visits once every one to two weeks, 24% weekly visits, and 3% twice per week. Thus it appears that the quantity of supervisor visits has decreased over the past fifty years. Second, in the initial study, 44% of the sample indicated they paid cooperating teachers for their participation. Of those who paid, the average stipend was $58, which translates to $375 in 2011 dollars (usinflation calculator.com). In the second study, the average stipend paid to cooperating teachers was $250. Although a larger percent of teachers likely are paid today, stipends have decreased significantly over time.

Third, in the original study, 85% of cooperating teachers had previously taken a college course in student teaching supervision. At the time, the most common methods used to train cooperating teachers included seminars (52%), workshops (33%) and conferences (31%). Overall, 27% of institutions offered a course in the supervision of student teaching at the time of the initial survey, with a mean enrollment of forty-six. Although there is no comparison data in the 2011 survey, formal training of cooperating teachers does not feature prominently in the current literature in student teaching. It is probably safe to assume that college courses geared toward student teaching supervision are not common today.

CHANGES IN SELECTION OF COOPERATING TEACHERS

Selection of cooperating teachers was also addressed in both studies, including desired characteristics. The initial study found that institutions of higher education desired teachers who were willing to serve in this role (45%), demonstrated good human relations skills (24%) and showed knowledge of teaching methodology (15%). When asked to what extent their cooperating teachers exemplified these competencies, the great majority of institutions (95%) responded at least "quite well." Although survey questions were not a perfect match, the most recent study collected similar data from the 77% of institutions of higher education that indicated seeking certain criteria in cooperating teachers. The most common requirement for cooperating teachers was at least three years of teaching experience (82%). Additionally, 38% of institutions required cooperating teachers to show good mentoring skills, and 28% had instituted some measure of effectiveness. These particular measures were not defined in the survey instrument.

The teaching experience requirements appear to represent a major shift in practice in the past fifty years. However, teaching effectiveness requirements for cooperating teachers appear to remain relatively uncommon. The research literature now recommends a minimum amount of experience and demonstrated classroom effectiveness (Greenberg et al., 2011). This change mirrors the general shift in philosophy and approach in the education field from process or inputs to outcomes or impact on K-12 students. Unfortunately, it is apparent from the recent study and from other reports in the professional literature that institutions of higher education still have little to no say in the selection of cooperating teachers (Greenberg et al., 2011).

ADDITIONAL STUDENT TEACHING PRACTICES

Several common practices referred to in the 1968 study are worth noting for their obsolescence today. First, historical student teaching admission requirements include several surprises. For example, well over half (60–65%) of all teacher preparation programs in the fifty states required student teachers to demonstrate emotional stability, physical fitness, and proficiency in "voice and speech." Fifty-four percent also required "personal-social-ethical fitness," which could be seen as similar to "professional dispositions" today.

Second, 23% of colleges and universities reported having laboratory schools. Although only approximately 35% of those institutions reported using these schools as a student teaching placement, with up four student teachers in a room simultaneously, the laboratory school structure had a significant impact on teacher education in past decades. Third, although a vaguely constructed question, 72% of institutions of higher education indicated that their student teachers "have some choice in [their student teaching assignments]." This finding is interesting given new research outcomes indicating that this type of choice could have a significant impact on later teacher quality (Goldhaber et al., 2017).

Fourth, the "Student Teaching Center" model discussed previously was referred to at different points in the study. To summarize, this model was originally proposed by the Joint Committee on State Responsibility for Student Teaching, a subcommittee formed by the National Education Association. It was a joint collaboration between a state's Department of Education, institutions of higher education, and K-12 schools. The model was spearheaded by two state-level boards, one on teacher education and one on student teaching, who would in turn develop a framework for implementation of local collaborative practices around student teaching. Interestingly, student teachers were assigned to centers instead of cooperating teachers, with the intent of broadening the student teaching experience (Hess, 1971). In the 1968 study, an average of 22% of institutions reported having teaching centers (Johnson, 1968). A 1969 doctoral thesis found that 40% of states indicated having at least one such center, with an average of five institutions of higher education in each state reporting using the model. The reported overall goal of these centers was to coordinate student teaching so as to fully utilize resources and provide for professional development needs of novice teachers. Objectives included the following:

1. To provide wide and varied direct experiences for the student teacher
2. To develop a program of both preservice and in-service education for teachers

3. To develop the role of the education center, coordinator, representative of the state, the college, and the school system
4. To clarify the roles of all other center personnel and
5. To explore state department involvement in the education center (Hess, 1971, p. 301)

Fifth, as discussed previously, reported methods used to train cooperating teachers were quite extensive in comparison to current practices. Over half of institutions reported using seminars to train cooperating teachers. Other common methods included workshops (33%), conferences (31%), formal coursework (27%), and a newsletter mailed to cooperating teachers (27%). Lesson common methods included sending cooperating teachers to state or national meetings. About one-quarter of institutions indicated they used "other" methods to train cooperating teachers, but these methods were not specified.

Finally, the benefits provided to cooperating teachers appear to have been more varied than the typical fee seen today. These benefits included library privileges (46%), "consultant services" (28%), "some free tuition" (25%). Less common benefits identified in the study included concert tickets, name in college catalog, athletic tickets, and college faculty status.

PROMISING PRACTICES

One can see why some claim that student teaching has remained unchanged in the past century, particularly with the same student teaching triad and general basic structures. Today's "innovations" typically involve concentrated efforts impacting selection or and/or support provided to at least one member of the triad, and/or deepening partnerships. If anything, basic practices and structures are more uniform and more rigid today than they were half a century ago.

In reviewing the professional literature in student teaching over the years, several practices and structures are worth discussing in a contemporary context, because of their alignment with what is currently considered to be best practice. These practices include (1) formal training for cooperating teachers and/or supervisors; (2) the use of technology to intensify supervision; (3) the Student Teaching Center concept; (4) providing choice in student teaching assignment; (5) using measures of classroom effectiveness to select cooperating teachers; and (6) expanding the triad to include more individuals in "boundary spanning" roles.

With respect to form training provided to cooperating teachers and supervisors, comparison of the two surveys pointed to a loosening of these offerings over the years, particularly with respect to college coursework in supervising student teachers. At one point, a great majority of cooperating teachers reported having taken such a course. Clarifying triad roles and ensuring a supportive experience appears to be critical to the success of the student teaching experience (Johnson & Napper-Owen, 2011), so creating and utilizing formal structures for this purpose could be considered a promising practice.

Second, the use of technology in intensifying supervision shows promise in the research (Schaefer & Ottley, 2018). As capabilities of technology and facility with its use continue to expand, the involvement of university personnel in experiences in external locations could be enhanced in ways that may not be foreseen at the current time. Bug-in-ear technology shows particular promise at the current time (see chapter 7), but this technology can be seen as only the beginning of possibility for the use of technology in supervision.

Third, although now obsolete, the history and practice of the Student Teaching Center concept should be explored further, particularly in light of new knowledge about crucial elements in student teaching practice. These elements include the importance of tight partnerships, standardization and understanding of roles in student teaching, careful selection of cooperating teachers, and careful placement of student teachings into particular communities. The Student Teaching Center concept was developed to focus a spotlight on student teaching and its importance to teacher development and quality, enhancing both university and K-12 settings. Such centers provided joint oversight and developed new structures to oversee the student teaching experience (Hess, 1971). Perhaps similar structures could be used to scale up positive practices in student teaching quickly and efficiently.

Fourth, recent research has underscored the importance of teacher candidate choice in student teaching assignment, due to the connection between later teacher effectiveness and the match between that assignment and later placement as a practicing teacher (Goldhaber et al., 2017). Taking choice into consideration when making student teaching assignments may have been more common in the past than it is today. Institutions of higher education may wish to reconsider the role of choice in this process and increased involvement of candidates, as well as K-12 partners in this process.

Fifth, using measures of teaching effectiveness to select cooperating teachers appears to be a relatively new development that should be encouraged. The professional literature has shown repeatedly that assigning student teachers to cooperating teachers who are themselves effective in the classroom is important to later teacher effectiveness. In fact, careful assignment of both teachers and schools appears to be important. Attention to these characteristics will be crucial as new research continues to uncover additional characteristics of settings that can be tied to later teacher success as well as to the success of the student teaching experience itself.

Finally, the recent push to enhance the quality of field experiences overall and student teaching experiences specifically does seem to have precipitated some changes, particularly with respect to adding a person to the traditional triad. Although quite varied as to the title, role, and employer, "clinical faculty" are intended to bridge the gap between K-12 and higher education (Zeichner, 2010). As such, these individuals have the potential to clarify the roles and responsibilities of the student teaching experiences and smooth the transition from student teacher to practicing teacher.

In conclusion, some of the promising practices highlighted in this chapter were common fifty years ago, and others are just emerging today. New research findings can shed a different light on some older practices that may still have the potential to move student teaching forward and have reinforced the potential value of other practices. These practices include more formal selection and supervision processes, the Teaching Center Concept, and creativity in "boundary spanning" in creating new and different connections between K-12 and teacher preparation. Reform is needed as those responsible for teacher preparation in both K-12 and higher education roles seek to close the research-to-practice gap in student teaching and to support teacher quality through carefully planned transitions for novice teachers.

Chapter 7

Innovation in Clinical Placement

Innovation in clinical placement in the past decade appears to have resulted directly from pressure from national organizations to intensify clinical experiences. Four major changes feature prominently in the professional literature and appear to be paving the way for long-lasting impact on the structure of student teaching. First, the coteaching model of student teaching, originating at St. Cloud State University in the mid-2000s as part of a U.S. Department of Education grant, has become widespread as a way to enhance classroom teaching, alleviate fears of student teachers lowering K-12 student achievement, and ensure the involvement of the cooperating teacher in the student teaching process. Second, full-year student teaching requirements have become popular across the United States. These full-year experiences attempt to emulate the successful, elite post–Baccalaureate "Teacher Residency" programs that have shown particular promise in preparing quality teachers (Wasburn-Moses, 2017). Third, technology-enhanced experiences have grown in an attempt to boost the quantity and quality of teacher candidate supervision, overcoming common time and distance constraints experienced by university supervisors. Finally, shared supervision has become common, with new roles inhabiting the "third space," coined by Zeichner (2010), the theoretical space between K-12 and higher education. As discussed in chapter 6, these new positions and roles often contain the terms "clinical" or "liaison." These individuals now play a critical role in student teaching and other field experiences at many institutions of higher education.

COTEACHING MODEL

The coteaching model can be seen as one of the most widespread recent developments in student teaching. Adopted by many states and institutions of higher education, this term now refers to a model in which the student teacher teaches alongside the cooperating teacher, rather than having the student teacher gradually take over the role of the cooperating teacher. Friend et al. (2015) note that the term originally (and still does) referred to a teaming approach between a general and special educator working collaboratively in an inclusive classroom so that the term can be unclear.

Baeten and Simons (2016) conducted a comprehensive review of the literature on the coteaching model in the student teaching experience. They identified three distinct models within the overarching coteaching framework. First, the "coplanning and coevaluation model" involves the student teacher and cooperating teacher (or mentor, in the author's words) in collaborating around lesson planning and evaluation, but only one of the partners has full responsibility for the delivery of that lesson. Second, the "assistant teaching mode" involves one of the partners taking the lead on the lesson while the other partner assists. These roles are then reversed. Third, in the "teaming model," collaboration is seen throughout lesson planning and delivery. The authors list the advantages and disadvantages of each model and identify four conditions for the success of the models overall. These four conditions involve adequate preparation for the new roles; emphasizing communication between the partners; encouraging relationships based on trust, respect, and honesty; and investing time in the model. In general, the advantages of the model include increasing support and professional growth on the part of both student teacher and cooperating teacher. More specifically, research has found that student teachers appear to gain support and show enhanced personal and professional growth over the traditional student teaching experience. Important conversations in the course of collaboration align thought with practice, modeling the complexities of teaching. Learning outcomes for student teachers include growth competence, or ability to self-reflect and use that reflection to improve teaching; adaptive teaching expertise, or adjusting teaching to fit student learning needs; and collaborative expertise, or working with others to develop professionally (Soslau et al., 2018). Disadvantages include barriers to communication, lack of equity and/or compatibility, and an increased workload. Overall, the authors concluded that the model does appear to be beneficial, and that advantages outweigh the disadvantages.

A later study also concluded that the model supports the learning of all involved in the process, including K-12 students (Soslau et al., 2018). A rare study focused on the impact of the coteaching model on K-12 students compared reading and math achievement scores in cotaught versus traditional student teaching classrooms. This study found that the youth in cotaught classrooms generally outperformed their peers (Bacharach et al., 2010).

YEAR-LONG STUDENT TEACHING

As interest in and support for increasing both quality and quantity of field experiences in teacher education has risen, the year-long student teaching assignment has become increasingly popular. Even though still relatively untested in the professional literature, this trend can still be viewed as an innovation due to its success in beginning to change the one-semester student teaching model that has remained in place for decades.

Although generally considered to be a recent phenomenon, the year-long student teaching experience is not a new concept in the United States. Overall, studies conducted over the past several decades have not found any difference between the traditional one-semester student teaching model and extended student teaching experiences, in the areas of classroom management or self-perceptions of teaching ability and beliefs. However, as is typical with research in teacher education, these studies were typically self-reports on single institutions with small sample sizes (Ronfeldt & Reininger, 2012).

One larger-scale study published in 2012 explored the relationship in length of student teaching experience to differences in later teacher quality, in addition to perceptions of efficacy, preparedness, and career plans. These authors collected data on four cohorts of over 1,000 student teachers in a single large urban district. Comparison of pre- and post-test data found the student teaching experience overall to have a positive and significant impact on teacher candidates, in terms of higher perceptions of preparedness, teaching efficacy, and reporting they were "somewhat more interested in working with underserved students" (p. 1103). The quality of the student teaching experience was also related positively to feelings of preparedness and to efficacy, as well as to teacher candidates' predictions for the longevity of their teaching careers. Interestingly, the magnitude of the impact of quality experiences was stronger in *shorter* teaching experiences in schools with more students of color. The quantity of the experience was unrelated to most of the variables included in this study, although it was weakly but positively related to perceptions of preparedness (Ronfeldt & Reininger, 2012).

In 2015, Arnett-Hartwick called extending student teaching a "national trend" (p. 42), although cautioned placing quantity over quality. Spooner et al. (2008) summarized the reasoning behind this movement: "Common sense indicates that candidates who receive increased amounts of field experience and mentoring opportunities to help them understand the realities of teaching are better prepared to deal with the complex realities of today's schools, classrooms, and students" (p. 1103). In sum, researchers tend to agree that users of this model should proceed with caution, as the evidence suggests that attention to quantity over quality, or increasing the amount of student teaching without changing its overall content to align with best practices, is unlikely to yield valuable results in terms of impact on future teacher quality.

TECHNOLOGY-ENHANCED SUPERVISION

In a 2009 review of the role of technology in field experiences in preservice teacher education, Hixon and So identified three types of field experiences. Only one of these types, Type 1, is applicable within a traditional student teaching setting, "concrete direct experience in reality." According to the authors, Type 1 tools "facilitate supervision, reflection, and/or communication" (p. 296). The tools evaluated in the professional literature are primarily real-time coaching and virtual supervision. They offer a more intensive way to supervise and communicate with teacher candidates in order to stimulate reflection on teaching. The authors of this review identified the general strengths and weaknesses of technology-enhanced field experience. Strengths relevant to Type 1 experiences include creating shared experiences and promoting reflection (Hixon & So, 2009).

Real-time coaching is a way to deliver performance-based feedback to teacher candidates in K-12 settings. A review of the literature on performance-based feedback uncovered specific characteristics of that feedback that were critical to meeting the criteria of an evidence-based practice in teacher education. Findings showed that the feedback provided must be positive, corrective, and specific. Previously, the only validated characteristic of effective feedback was immediacy (Scheeler et al., 2004). The traditional way performance feedback is delivered to teacher candidates is through conferencing, typically after a formal observation by a supervisor. Throughout the years, many models of delivering performance feedback have been researched within this face to face model, primarily because of its potential for enhancing teacher performance. However, these models often fail to reach their potential because of the delay in time between the delivery of the lesson and the time the feedback is presented to the teacher candidate, typically in a conference. This delay then results in loss of the most effective elements of the feedback—namely, "immediacy, clarity, consistency, and relevance to the context" (Shaefer & Ottley, 2018, p. 247).

Technology provides a way to avoid these limitations of traditional feedback. Although various types of technology have been used to deliver feedback to teacher candidates as they are engaging in instruction in the field,

"Bug-in-ear" technology is used most widely (Rock et al., 2009; Schaefer & Ottley, 2018). This technology is used to connect theory in practice for teacher candidates. It allows them to apply the knowledge and skills they have gained in their preparation programs in real-life settings, in a manner that can result in immediate change (Scheeler, 2007). Additionally, teacher candidates can see the immediate impact of changes in their own behavior on K-12 learners (Odom et al., 2005). In sum, the ultimate goal of use of bug-in-ear technology is faster and stronger acquisition of effective teaching behaviors (Schaefer & Ottley, 2018).

Although widely considered a promising practice in the area of supervision in teacher preparation, limitations in the research still prohibit conclusive evidence on the use of this technology. Strong on effectiveness and feasibility are missing. Additionally, bug-in-ear feedback was often combined with other types of feedback in the professional literature, making conclusions about its effectiveness challenging, if not impossible. However, in 2017 Schaefer and Ottley undertook a comprehensive review of the literature on the use of bug-in-ear technology and compared the evidence on effectiveness to the standards adopted by What Works Clearinghouse (WWC). Their goals were to investigate effectiveness, feasibility, and satisfaction on participation of both supervisor and supervisee. Seventeen articles met their inclusion criteria for analysis, involving sixty-six total practitioners. Results indicated that providing immediate performance feedback through the use of bug-in-ear technology did meet the criteria for being considered an evidence-based practice in changing teaching behaviors. They concluded that this technology showed promise for producing lasting (generalized) behavior change, even in new teaching environments. Feasibility and satisfaction were rated highly as well (Schaefer & Ottley, 2018).

VIRTUAL SUPERVISION

Virtual supervision is defined as "using distance education methods (synchronous or asynchronous) to supervise student teachers as a supplemental approach to face to face supervision" (Liu et al., 2018, p. 2). Virtual supervision dates back more than twenty years and has a long history of experimentation using a multitude of technologies and strategies, most often in rural areas where direct supervision is difficult. Early efforts in this field tended to be asynchronous and accomplished through the use of email, online discussion boards, and video submitted at a later date. Later, the use of synchronous technology to supervise teacher candidates in the field in real time began to appear in the professional literature (Liu et al., 2018).

Some researchers see great promise in the use of these technologies in supplementing or even replacing on-the-ground supervisors, particularly university-based supervisors. Not only does the strategy solve problems of distance and expense of traditional supervision, but it could allow for more intensive contact between teacher candidates and supervisors, more opportunities for reflection and feedback, and more awareness of issues in rural education (Billingsley et al., 2018; Schmidt et al., 2015).

However, issues with the field and past research make evaluation of these technologies difficult. First, like many areas in teacher education, the available literature often employs a weak research design, including lack of a control group, reliance on perception measures or other indirect measures, and/or use of small sample sizes, often confined to a single institution of higher education. Second, the large variance in technologies utilized and the ways in which these technologies provide supervision vary widely, making across-study comparison difficult (Billingsley et al., 2018; Schmidt et al., 2015). Third, definitions of both "virtual" and "supervision" have been applied inconsistently throughout the professional literature, resulting in studies that equate (for example) the use of email communication with synchronous videoconferencing. Finally, this field tends to be dominated by the technology side, placing descriptions of the technology itself and its strengths and barriers over outcome research. All of these issues are common in a relatively new field, particularly one involving ever-changing platforms that in turn change the potential for delivery of the supervision (Liu et al., 2018).

Despite these challenges, particularly design flaws and a constantly changing field, some studies have shown promise in the use of virtual supervision in field experience, in terms of comparing effectiveness to face to face models, and solving common problems involving distance. One study compared the outcomes of virtual supervision by supervisors in a traditional university with those in an online university. Supervisors were asked to respond to surveys and interviews and provide additional data on teacher candidates, including grades and email communication. Authors found significant differences in the effectiveness of the virtual supervision based on "receptivity of the use of the supervision [model] by the supervisor" (Schwartz-Bechet, 2014, p. 10). The authors also found this perception transferred to teacher candidates, in that the teacher candidates assigned to supervisors who embraced and initiated the use of the technology were more successful, both in the use of the technology itself and in the quality of their lessons. Implications included a strong need for training and support in the use of technology on the part of supervisors (Schwartz-Bechet, 2014).

Another study related specifically to the virtual supervision of student teachers in rural areas. Although conducted within one Midwest University, this study triangulated data from multiple sources, including observation, post-conference videos, and pre-post interviews with the student teacher, cooperating teacher, supervisor, principal, and superintendent. The research reinforced the conclusion of others that the technology has the potential to transform supervision in rural areas, particularly with respect to building community and partnerships and reducing isolation. Professional development for both teacher candidates and cooperating teachers was enhanced. The authors concluded their study by providing practical considerations for implementation, including the need to build trust, plan for technology costs and glitches, and to prioritize the learning of K-12 students (Liu et al., 2018).

"THIRD SPACE" SUPERVISION

"Third space supervision" involves additions or changes to the traditional triad of student teacher, cooperating teacher, and university supervisor. For example, Burns et al. (2016) found a significant expansion of roles and even new positions now involved in teacher candidate supervision, prompting them to conclude that "if multiple individuals who span the boundaries of schools and universities are needed to enact [teacher candidate] supervision in clinically-rich contexts, then the use of the term *university supervisor* to describe their role seems inaccurate and exclusionary" (p. 422). The authors also identify various titles of these new boundary spanners, as discussed previously, who serve as a "third space" dweller in the words of Zeichner (2010).

Unfortunately, the professional literature is unclear and varied with respect to descriptions of the specific roles of those considered to be "boundary spanners." Much of this work focuses on a single teacher preparation program / or the role of a specific supervisor functioning outside the traditional triad. Williams (2014) studied eighteen teacher candidates working in three countries, investigating the roles of those assigned to supervise these candidates in the field. Participants reported shifting identities and the need to manage relationships within and across the complex environments of higher education and K-12 education. Allen et al. (2014) identified a fourth member of the triad within a specific university's setting. This "clinical instructor" was described as a site-based university teacher educator who supported the triad in various ways, including providing targeted professional development for each of the members of the triad. These reports on practice are examples of changing roles in supervision. Overarching models of how these individuals and roles have affected the concept of the triad remain lacking from the professional literature. The relative newness of the positions may contribute to the lack of agreement and specificity surrounding titles and roles. Burns et al. (2016) speculated that multiple people might be sharing the responsibility for

supervising clinical experiences, adding to the lack of clarity in the professional literature.

In conclusion, despite a long history of myriad challenges, it appears that
the structure of student teaching may be changing and even possibly moving away from the traditional triad of student teacher, cooperating teacher,
and university supervisor. New roles are developing, involving new and
more intensive types of support, more and different individuals involved in
the process, different types of interaction/communication, and new methods
of professional development for all stakeholders. Boundary spanners help
connect K-12 and teacher preparation. Although they still face multiple challenges, they are helping to define the "third space" in teacher education and
have the potential to create new directions for both teacher education more
broadly and student teaching specifically (Zeichner, 2010).

Chapter 8

Principles for Practice

Clearly, the time is right for a sea change in clinical placement. Theory, research, and popular thought have coalesced around the need to rethink the role of clinical experience in preparing teachers, with the K-12 and higher education communities collaborating around the work of preparing teachers for classroom and community contexts. Student teaching is a perfect place to begin because of its universality and intensity. The work of the triad—the student teacher, cooperating teacher, and university supervisor—is at the epicenter of these contexts. Although this basic structure and its myriad challenges have remained unchanged for decades, the current climate surrounding teacher preparation has the promise to breathe new life into what many see as stagnant roles.

Much thought and work have gone into documenting these long-standing barriers to achieve the goals for student teaching, most notably raising teacher effectiveness. These barriers include low rewards and recognition for clinical work across K-12 and higher education settings, lack of compelling data-based research on crucial elements of teacher preparation tied to youth outcomes, and the historical disconnect between K-12 and higher education settings and structures. Comparisons across time have shown both consistency and change in various aspects of student teaching.

Despite these obstacles, we believe that student teaching as a nearly universal structure in teacher preparation programs holds promise as the catalyst to demonstrable, lasting change in the field of teacher preparation. We provide three reasons for this conclusion:

1. Student teaching is remarkably common and uniform across the United States. It has high visibility among the larger school community, and its basic structure is well-documented (i.e., the triad). Its long-lasting

standing indicates it is unlikely to go away soon, even with recent innovation.

2. Student teaching is already widely recognized and supported in K-12 and higher education settings, albeit poorly in many cases. Despite the challenges outlined above, structures are already in place in both settings that support these roles, and resources (however minimal) devoted to maintaining this structure.

3. Student teaching is often identified as the single most important facet of teacher preparation, in terms of its impact on teacher candidates. Thus, if an institution of higher education or K-12 partner manages to modify the student teaching experience to increate alignment with evidence-based practices, the impact on teacher preparation overall will be greater than making other programmatic changes, such as changes to coursework or to other field experiences.

Below we provide four principles for practice in student teaching, resting on the premise outlined above that reform in student teaching can serve as a gateway to comprehensive redesign of teacher preparation. Strengthening student teaching could accomplish the mutually agreed-upon goals that have surfaced multiple times in the history of teacher preparation yet not accomplished in a widespread, consistent manner that can be documented. These principles of practice are designed to meet both broad and specific goals of student teaching.

For example, reform of student teaching will create strong, mutually beneficial partnerships. Changes in student teaching cannot happen in a vacuum. It must include both K-12 and higher education partners, and as each partner seeks to meet its goals, lasting change would need to mutually beneficial. The principles address redesign of professional development within the context of strengthening partnerships. Partners will each have a role in the provision of the professional development, where typically, they operate as separate systems in K-12 and university environments.

Further, a concerted effort to change student teaching as a well-recognized entity in education will at very least raise visibility and awareness, if not the status of the roles surrounding the student teaching experience. As more individuals are involved in student teaching in different ways, new roles will be created for various stakeholders, both inside and outside the traditional triad. Finally, efforts to enhance student teaching as a crucial element of the overall teacher preparation program will push on the misalignment between course- and fieldwork that is so often referred to in the professional literature. K-12 and higher education partners will rethink and attempt to align needs and values through the planning process. The ensuing discussions could represent a first step in addressing this gap.

The principles for practice were developed using the available research literature in both student teaching particularly and practices in teacher preparation more broadly. Particular emphasis was given to practices shown to impact youth outcomes after the student teacher became a practicing teacher wherever possible, the gold standard in this type of research. Practicality and succinctness were also important concepts in the development of the principles, because of the need for reform efforts to be resource-efficient, simple, focused, and generally attainable by personnel with extremely limited time and resources to devote to creating new structures. In fact, considerable effort was devoted to modifying and/or replacing traditional structures where possible, rather than adding new ones.

The following section of this text is devoted to the planning, implementation, and evaluation process to assist K-12 and higher education partners in putting these principles into practice in real-world settings. Chapter 9 provides partners with steps needed to accomplish transformation in student teaching, based upon the principles presented. Chapter 10 expands upon these steps by describing how the redesign of student teaching can serve as a springboard or first step to complete redesign of teacher preparation programs.

COMMON PHILOSOPHY

Arguably, the single greatest barrier to achieving high-quality teacher preparation is the complex and deeply rooted separation between traditional higher education teacher preparation and the daily work of K-12 schools. This physical and philosophical separation has led to a multitude of challenges addressed in this text, including the much-discussed research-to-practice gap in teaching practices as well as the gap between course- and fieldwork in teacher preparation.

Establishing common philosophies can be seen as a way to begin to bridge this gap. Before common philosophies can be articulated, though, each partner needs to ask and answer questions about its own philosophy, and determining how that philosophy is expressed through daily teaching practices, whether that be K-12 or higher education. Mission and vision statements can assist in this work but are notorious for their vague wording and lack of follow-through in practice. Further, many large organizations can have difficulty articulating common approaches or beliefs even among their own constituents, so this work needs to occur first.

The need for common philosophies is well supported in the research literature around the creation of partnerships in support of strengthening teaching and teacher preparation. For example, AACTE's Clinical Practice Commission's Manifesto, "A Pivot toward Clinical Practice, Its

Lexicon, and the Renewal of Educator Preparation" (AACTE, 2018) presents ten "Proclamations and Tenets for Highly Effective Clinical Educator Preparation." The goal of this document is "to embrace a common lexicon and a shared understanding of evidence-based practices for embedding teacher preparation in the K-12 environment" (p. 2). This shared understanding of what works in teaching and learning has long been seen as a pivotal foundation to strong partnership (e.g., Cochran-Smith & Zeichner, 2005; Hollins, 2015; Wilson et al., 2001).

It may be helpful to think of the work of identifying and integrating common philosophies as similar to the work involved in developing Multi-Tiered Systems of Support (MTSS) in K-12 schools. Both of these initiatives are designed to look different in various school contexts by meeting local needs. However, the work always begins by gathering diverse stakeholders in order to develop shared principles and values. These activities are fundamental to achieving fidelity in implementation, as these systems rely on continuity of practices across settings. For example, MTSS planning often involves the development of schoolwide rules, progress monitoring, and common reward systems (Lane et al., 2013). With respect to teacher preparation, a clear vision of good teaching practices should be evident across courses within a single program, and both course- and fieldwork should build on each other in a developmental process (Cochran-Smith & Zeichner, 2000). Once these processes determine philosophies within a system, the partners can meet to generate the common vision.

Essential elements that support the principle of common philosophies include the following:

1. A concerted effort to include all stakeholders in the development of the philosophies, such as faculty, administrators, students, alumni, and support staff;
2. Documentation of specific practices by both partners that can be used as examples to describe what the philosophy looks like in practice;
3. Identification of a smaller working group to continue the work of the larger team; and
4. Creation of a concise, practical statement that can guide future work as the partnership solidifies and expands.

The goal of generating a common philosophy is to develop connections between K-12 and higher education that help guide the daily work of both systems, instead of creating an add-on to other mission, vision, and/or goal statements. The philosophy will not be a perfect match or overlap completely with existing statements, but will nevertheless serve as a guide in setting goals and learner outcomes and determining new roles for clinical partners.

Partners will need to negotiate the work of creating statements that are neither too broad nor too narrow in scope, aiming for a few basic, practical principles that can be identified in action in the classroom.

RESEARCH GROUNDED MATCHMAKING

Matchmaking refers to deliberate, mutual planning on the part of both higher education and K-12 partners to place specific teacher candidates in specific classrooms in specific districts. Currently, higher education appears to be involved in this process only about half of the time, despite its importance (Greenberg et al., 2011). Further, although conducted in good faith, matchmaking too often is based on the perceptions and biases of one individual or rules unrelated to the research-based practices that are known to be related to later teacher quality. An example of matchmaking that aligns with research outcomes is as follows. Higher education representatives meet with school partners each semester with information about each teacher candidate, such as strengths and needs, resume, desired placement, and future goals, including a description of the type of setting(s) in which the candidate wishes to be employed after graduation. K-12 partners come to the table with their own list of teachers, both qualified and willing to serve as cooperating teachers. Both teacher candidates and practicing teachers need to have met mutually determined and publicized quality standards, including (for teachers) evidence of effectiveness in the classroom and evidence of mentoring ability. The partners then proceed to make matches between teacher candidates and cooperating teachers. Common practices to assist in this type of matchmaking include having the potential cooperating teachers and/or school administrators interview teacher candidates, and requiring teacher candidates to spend time in the cooperating teachers' classrooms working with K-12 students before the match is finalized.

To highlight the importance of careful matchmaking, about 15% of current teachers were hired into the same school in which they student taught, and about 40% hired into the same district (Krieg et al., 2016). Further, new research shows a "strong inverse relationship between the proportion of teachers in schools or districts that host a student teacher and the likelihood that those schools and districts rely on emergency credentialed teachers to staff classrooms" (Goldhaber et al., 2019, p. 2). Even when controlling for multiple observable school variables (e.g., SES, urbanicity, distance to teacher preparation program), researchers found that hosting student teachers is a possible way to lower a schools' reliance on teachers with emergency credentials. The study "adds the next brick to the empirical wall that could eventually support a focus on student teaching placements as a policy level for addressing regional teacher shortages" (Goldhaber et al., 2019, p. 16).

Other research shows compelling evidence that the match between student teacher placement and later school of employment in terms of youth demographics is related to stronger outcomes for the student teacher's future students. This finding means that teachers hired into schools that are similar demographically to the schools in which they student taught are more effective teachers than those without this close match (Boyd et al., 2017). Taken together, the evidence suggests strongly that the entire educational system can benefit significantly from careful matchmaking.

Further, significant research has supported the need for careful selection of both cooperating teachers and university supervisors, to ensure that they are both effective teachers and effective mentors (Greenberg et al., 2012). This principle also addresses several of the major concerns outlined by Greenberg et al. (2012) at the conclusion of their national survey of student teaching practices, including the misalignment of teacher supply and demand, the lack of control of institutions of higher education over student teaching placements, and the need to "raise the bar" for entry into and exit from student teaching.

In sum, specific elements supporting the principle on matchmaking includethe following:

1. Aligning student teaching placements with desired future teaching positions;
2. Creating and publicizing a shared (across K-12 and higher education) list of qualifications for student teachers, cooperating teachers, and university supervisors;
3. Making a careful match for each triad, taking into account desired personal and professional characteristics; and
4. Making matches a shared responsibility between partners.

TRIAD ROLE CLARITY

Triad role clarity refers to identifying and implementing specific expectations for each of the central actors in student teaching—the student teacher, cooperating teacher, and university supervisor. The vision for triad role clarity is for each of the individuals of the triad to enter the student teaching experience with specific knowledge about the goals of the experience and expectations for their roles, including expected processes (e.g., observations, feedback sessions) and outputs. For example, an institution of higher education might require five-hour-long visits by the student teaching supervisor, each followed by a thirty-minute conference with each member of the triad, with specific forms to be completed and turned in within a week of the visit. These goals and expectations should be developed mutually by institutions of higher education and partner districts, aligned with predetermined goals, and contain a plan for monitoring outcomes. Further, the need for a supportive student teaching experience should be evident throughout the plan, as aligned with the research literature. For example, partners should ensure time for planning, discussion, and debriefing, as well as attention to strengthening teaching, experiencing success, and taking time to decompress. Finally, ongoing attention to the health of the triad's relationship would also be apparent.

The need for role clarity is a major theme in the extensive literature on the supervision of field and clinical experiences. This issue was summarized well by Johnson and Napper-Owen (2011), who documented common issues with supervision that led to a lack of fulfillment of the student teaching experience as an opportunity for growth in teacher effectiveness. These issues include a general lack of understanding of roles and lack of a shared vision of the goal(s) of the experience, despite each actor acting in good faith. The long-lasting value of a supportive student teaching experience is also a common theme in the research literature (Boyd et al., 2009). In fact, the link was made between this particular quality of the experience and later teacher attrition (Ronfeldt, 2012). Research also points to the need for more supportive student teaching experiences to act as a "buffer" against the well-documented drop in efficacy that accompanies the first year of teaching. Essential elements that support the principle of triad role clarity are as follows:

1. Developing mutual goals/themes to guide the student teaching experience and conveying those goals to all stakeholders;
2. Developing mutually agreed upon expectations for the roles of each individual in the triad, including processes and outcomes (e.g., number of visits and conferences, required documentation);
3. Determining specific ways in which the triad can collaborate to ensure that the student teaching experience is supportive; and
4. Determining plans for oversight and guidance of the triad to ensure the health of the relationship and that goals are met.

MUTUAL PROFESSIONAL DEVELOPMENT

Mutual professional development presumes a vision that all stakeholders gain knowledge and skill from the student teaching experience. A systemic goal of implementing this type of professional development is that it would change the culture of student teaching and use partnership as an opportunity for authentic growth within an already existing system. As partnerships around student teaching expand, the goal is to grow the visibility of new roles, which will hopefully increase the willingness of effective teachers to serve as cooperating teachers.

The vision of mutual professional development is quite simple. Partners agree on a broad theme to extend student teachers' learning, such as data-based reading intervention, schoolwide behavior supports, or the use of mindfulness techniques in the classroom. This theme should be tied to both partners' programmatic goals and be supported by data. Partners then design professional development around this goal in ways that align with best practice research in professional development (i.e., sustained, supported, teacher-led study with guided follow-through and attention to assessment of impact on youth). The plan should take into account formal as well as informal professional development needs, such as offering a masters-level course for teachers or research opportunities for faculty. Involving the student teachers as well as the other members of the triad as partners in creating the professional development content and structures develops a sense of ownership and reinforces their new professional identity as a teacher (Valencia et al., 2009). This principle is bolstered by the research in several areas, including the previously discussed need for role clarity and alignment among the student teaching triad.

Rust and Clift (2015) point out that despite the best intentions of those striving to intensify and enhance clinical placements, the outcomes of those placements will not improve unless the placements are focused. The authors define "focused clinical practice" as "practice in which practitioners are actively studying their own actions and impact alongside other practitioners" (p. 49). This professional dialogue requires jointly developed goals and is unique to each partnership. It pushes all parties to extend and evaluate their work in a team, one of the primary goals for student teaching that often goes unrealized due to traditional structural limitations (Johnson & Napper-Owen, 2011).

The other body of research supporting this principle is in the area of professional development for teachers. Unfortunately, traditional "one-shot" professional development is notoriously unsuccessful at making a significant, long-lasting impact on teaching and learning. Researchers tend to agree that professional development needs to change in specific ways, but supporting a grass roots carefully designed and sustained program of inquiry with ongoing support requires significant commitment of time and resources. However, this is where the partnership can step in by harnessing the expertise of both university and school personnel. Together this team possesses a deep understanding of research and practice, as well as the needs, goals, and strengths of the school and community.

In sum, mutual professional development needs to contain the following elements:

1. Development of a mutually agreed-upon theme, based around needs grounded in local data
2. Organization of activities that fit within the established work of the triad
3. Grassroots, sustained, supported, and carefully evaluated elements that constitute best practice in professional development for educators and
4. Inclusion of all stakeholders

Chapter 9

First Steps

Typically, change in both K-12 and higher education is slow. Faculty, staff, and administration are already overburdened with administrative tasks and increasing requirements for compliance. When these two different and bulky systems attempt to collaborate around change, that change can be even slower and often seem to carry an even larger administrative burden, particularly when safety, permissions, and legal agreements become factors. The challenge is to work smarter, and not harder.

This chapter is all about working smarter by starting small, particularly for those institutions not able to make an immediate, sweeping commitment to revamping student teaching. It provides questions to ask and topics to discuss with stakeholders to become more intentional about the entire structure of student teaching, one principle and one semester at a time.

To begin, select one principle from chapter 8: (1) common philosophy, (2) research-ground matchmaking, (3) triad role clarity, or (4) mutual professional development. Be sure to select the principle you believe your institution and partners are most ready to consider and implement. For example, if you have strong supervisors, select triad role clarity. If school partners are asking to deepen involvement, select mutual professional development. If you are beginning your work with a new school partner, begin by addressing philosophy. Weighing the relative strengths of stakeholders with respect to your partnership(s) will assist you in making decisions about where to start and how to proceed.

When you have selected one principle, skip to the relevant section of this chapter to outline your first steps and create goals for the upcoming semesters, one step at a time. It is important to note that although the discussion refers only to one school partner, more than one will probably be involved. The steps are identical, but it will take additional thought and time to select participating stakeholders, bring them together, and determine a course of action. The first steps presented under each principle are guided by the following components:

1. Strengthening Partnerships: All work directed toward closing the research-to-practice gap in student teaching necessitates strengthening partnerships, and each principle outlined in chapter 8 requires input from both K-12 and higher education. These partnerships must be ongoing and will evolve over time. Initial thought and action are addressed directly below, but the partnership and action steps will change each semester as more information and feedback derived from the implementation of the changes filter through partners. Developing strong and well-defined policies and structures is a must in order to sustain this work.

2. Using Clinical Educators More Intentionally: As discussed previously, the term "clinical educators" has multiple equivalents, yet remains difficult to define precisely because of the varied and relatively new nature of the position(s). Here, we rely on a simple definition of "boundary spanner" as an individual whose work is in both K-12 and higher education settings and concentrates on the preparation of teachers. Many partnerships are quite creative in their planning for and use of clinical educators. Even if your partnership has not added individuals to the triad, enhancing student teaching will necessitate rethinking and expanding traditional roles around the student teaching experience.

3. Intensifying Connections Between Course- and Fieldwork: Traditionally, the student teaching semester does not involve coursework, most often intentionally so that student teachers are not overburdened and can spend 100% of their time focused on student teaching rather than on college coursework. However, one could argue that this deliberate separation contributes to the disconnect between student teaching and the remainder of the teacher candidate's program of study. In the discussion of taking the first steps for each principle, ideas are presented to begin to connect this work on student teaching with the remainder of the teacher preparation program.

Below each principle introduced in the previous chapter is organized by common steps. The steps include (1) identifying stakeholders; (2) outlining research findings; (3) listing benefits; (4) meeting of stakeholders; (5) developing a written action plan, including principles, a common plan, and follow-up; (6) future plans with examples; and (7) making connections to coursework. Plans by semester are separated from the action plan because they involve future steps, which are more tentative, whereas the action plan is immediate. These steps cover the typical cycle of innovation, from planning to implementation to evaluation to revisiting the innovation and making modifications based on that analysis.

COMMON PHILOSOPHY

It makes sense to begin planning for expanded partnership work around student teaching by articulating a common philosophy to guide the experience. Although the philosophy is focused on student teaching, the action steps associated with this principle involve aligning the student teaching experience with the new philosophy. This step will also simplify later program alignment.

1. Identify Stakeholders: Beginning with this principle may involve identifying a wider stakeholder base, as it involves faculty, staff, students and administration associated with student teaching in order to provide expertise. Administrators involved in student teaching may include K-12 central office personnel as well as higher education leaders (e.g., deans, field directors). Representation from the student teaching triad of student teachers, cooperating teachers, and university supervisors is essential. In preparation for the meeting, locate existing statements about the purpose of student teaching (e.g., in a handbook or online), as well as broader mission/vision statements written to govern the work of each entity at the table.
2. Outline Research Findings: Below are some resources to consult when summarizing work in the importance of common philosophies in partnership:

   Zeichner, K. M. (2010). Rethinking the connections between campus courses and field experiences in college- and university-based teacher education. *Journal of Teacher Education, 61*(1–2), 89–99.
   American Association of Colleges for Teacher Education. (2018). *A pivot toward clinical practice, its lexicon, and the renewal of educator preparation.* Washington, D.C.: AACTE.

   The outline should be brief (no more than one to two paragraphs), and bullet points are helpful. The research findings and list of benefits below should be presented at the stakeholder meeting in no more than one single-sided page.
3. List Benefits: Benefits should be listed in table or bullet point form and should include all parties (e.g., school, district, university).
4. Meeting of Stakeholders: This meeting should follow a clear and concise agenda, including the elements below. The meeting may get unwieldy

with a large number of participants, so you may have to weigh the need for broad participation against this factor when determining the list of invitees.

5. Developing a Written Action Plan: The Action Plan, which will be the written goal of the stakeholder meeting, involves three items: (1) the philosophy itself, (2) the communication plan, and (3) follow-up. There should be no more than three principles when developing a common philosophy. One sentence may in fact be sufficient, provided it is specific enough so as to lead to changes in classroom practices. For example, the group may choose to focus student teaching on meeting school goals in reading intervention, behavior support, technology, or mental health supports for K-12 learners. It may focus on various aspects of teacher development, such as the use of feedback, culturally responsive teaching practices, or various high leverage practices for learners at risk. This type of statement is much more practical and specific than a typical philosophy, with its more amorphous goals, such as "becoming lifelong learners" or "reach all students."

   A communication plan around a common philosophy can vary widely depending on the number of student teachers in a building or district. Of importance is to determine relatively soon after implementation what the philosophy looks like in practice and how implementation may vary across triads and even across buildings and districts. Of course, uniformity is not required or even necessarily desired, but some common threads are important to maintain the focus of the philosophy. Follow-up around the philosophy is relatively simple despite the number of people involved. Some type of check-in, face to face or virtual, is recommended at least once per semester in order to document interpretation of the philosophy and how to move forward based upon this reality. Evaluation based on some type of data related to the philosophy is important to consider and determine before implementation. Documenting these outcome(s) and communicating them to all stakeholders will ensure the continuation of the work, and therefore strengthening of the partnership.

6. Future Steps: Future steps should be labeled by semester or year. As the variability in implementation becomes apparent as the data are examined. Stakeholders can determine which elements they may find particularly valuable and wish to include in future plans. As written plans outline the next steps, particularly with respect to connections to coursework discussed below, you will find the other three principles presented in chapter 8 coming into play. For example, putting a philosophy of student teaching into practice necessitates clarifying roles and will probably involve more concentrated professional development activities. Examples of future steps may include expanding a certain activity to

additional classrooms, switching goals, requiring additional data collection on the part of the student teacher, or revising the student teaching evaluation process.

7. Making Connections to Coursework: As previously stated, articulating a common philosophy can be a precursor to much larger transformation in teacher education. Once the philosophy is set and goals are being met, ask yourself how teacher candidates can be better prepared to work within this framework before beginning student teaching. Likely multiple districts are involved with one university's students teaching program, so how can these districts tap into the work that has already been done? How can the work be used to inform pre-student teaching practica and specific courses in content and/or pedagogy? This next step is a significant undertaking, but one that could have a far-reaching impact in narrowing the gap between course- and fieldwork that too often remains unaddressed.

RESEARCH GROUNDED MATCHMAKING

If you begin your work with more intentional matchmaking between student teachers and cooperating teachers, schools, and districts, your efforts should begin to pay off almost immediately. Not only will you be providing a more meaningful and personalized student teaching experience, but districts should reap benefits in the form of short- and long-term job placement and staffing solutions. You will need to determine how to change the structure and interactions around student teaching assignments without significantly increasing administrative burdens, with the goal of creating more engaged partners through more intentional planning.

1. Identify Stakeholders: This step is fairly simple because the primary stakeholders are those currently involved in making student teaching placements for a building or district, plus student teacher and cooperating teacher representatives. These additional two groups should be included because more intentional matchmaking will take into account the perspectives and wishes of student teachers, and cooperating teachers may have more input in selection than in the traditional selection. Also, be sure to consider whether others need to be included in order to meet the goal, for example, building-level administrators or university faculty.

2. Outline Research Findings: The research findings in this area are recent but very strong. The latest studies in this area can be downloaded from caldercouncil.org. Findings can be outlined quite simply; findings and benefits below should both be summarized in one-half to one page total.

3. List Benefits: Benefits should be organized into several categories, including higher education, student teacher, school, and district. Many parties benefit from more intentional matchmaking for student teaching, hopefully including future students taught by the former student teacher. As stated above, districts benefit from more careful selection most directly, particularly in that they will be more likely to hire teachers they have had the opportunity to preselect.

4. Meeting of Stakeholders: The timing of this meeting needs to be determined carefully so as to align with the existing student teaching matchmaking timetable. Plan for plenty of extra time for what will be a more complex and in-depth process that may involve more individuals and possibly events such as interviewing. During the meeting, it will be important to determine the amount of change desired immediately and over time. Change could start small, such as simply having student teachers fill out a form indicating the geographic area and type of district in which they see themselves working in the future. Conversely, stakeholders could set up a comprehensive vetting and matching system immediately, involving multiple face-to-face meetings and various parties with various roles.

5. Developing a Written Action Plan: Rather than articulating principles, the stakeholders need to articulate how matches will be made (see above). What will the process look like and who will be involved at each stage? In this case, the principles and communication plans are one and the same. Who will have a say at each level might be challenging to determine and might need to be revisited at a future date. Written follow-up is a part of this particular plan that may be easy to overlook once the plan has been followed and matches are made for the first group. Care needs to be taken to solicit input from those most impacted by the change in matchmaking procedure, including members of the triad as well as building administrators. Check to see if data are already being collected on satisfaction with student teaching placements from the perspectives of various stakeholders. If so, a simple comparison can be made. Planning to follow up with former teachers is challenging even in structured research studies. It would be a long-term benefit to attempt to track where student teachers take their first positions in comparison to their student teaching assignments. Therefore, written follow-up may be more complex, involving data collection and analysis to inform future practice.

6. Future Steps: Future steps will differ greatly depending upon the length of the first step taken. Future steps may simply involve data analysis, or it may involve increasing efforts each semester to expand adherence research-based principles of matchmaking. It may involve working with an increasing number of districts on the same plan. In any case, follow

through in determining and analyzing impact is essential to moving forward with this principle.

7. Making Connections to Coursework: Connections to coursework are not as obvious for the matchmaking principle but are nevertheless important. Typical preservice coursework in teacher education does not leave room for much exploration of teacher candidates' desires in their future teaching positions, despite the fact that they are likely to be developing these desires through course- and fieldwork. Thus connections to coursework mean determining critical places in that coursework to offer that opportunity to explore and make explicit the importance of those desires in student teaching placement and their future career. Spending some time discussing these issues could be empowering for teacher candidates in realizing they have some control over their immediate and long-term future.

TRIAD ROLE CLARITY

Another simple starting point in transforming student teaching involves clarifying the roles of each member of the triad. Deliberating on these roles and how they are carried out in practice can lead the way forward in narrowing the research-to-practice gap. Some claim that practices in student teaching have remained virtually unchanged over the past century. This phenomenon only occurs because the individuals involved are not able to take the time to deliberate, plan for change, and evaluate outcomes to inform future practice.

1. Identify Stakeholders: Stakeholders are not difficult to locate when addressing this principle. In this case, the "Triad" refers to the student teacher, the cooperating teacher, and the university supervisor. K-12 administrators and anyone else serving the triad in the schools or at the university should also be included in the initial meeting. In particular, seek out any "boundary spanners" as defined in the previous chapter for their particular knowledge in comparing the two different systems in practice.

2. Outline Research Findings: As reported previously, the lack of role clarity, currently and historically, has led to negative outcomes for the student teaching experience. Below are recommended articles to consider in summarizing findings to present to the stakeholders. A half-page bulleted list of common challenges would be helpful to guide the team's work:

Johnson, I. L., and Napper-Owen, G. (2011). The importance of role perceptions in the student teaching triad. *Physical Educator, 68*(1), 44–56.

Valencia, S. W., Martin, S. D., Place, N. A., and Grossman, P. (2009). Complex interactions in student teaching: Lost opportunities for learning. *Journal of Teacher Education, 60*(3), 304–322.

3. List Benefits: Benefits of the work can also be gleaned from the research literature. On the bottom half of the page, list benefits to each stakeholder: student teacher, cooperating teacher, university supervisor, and others such as administrators at school or university. Be sure to include the important that clarifying roles can also save administrator time in terms of solving problems later on.

Burns, R. W., Jacobs, J., and Yendol-Hoppey, D. (2016). The changing nature of the role of the university supervisor and function of preservice teacher supervision in an era of clinically rich practice. *Action in Teacher Education, 38*(4), 410–425.

4. Meeting of Stakeholders: In addition to reporting the research findings and benefits of the work, the meeting of stakeholders has a simple agenda to clarify the roles of the student teaching triad, as well as any other individuals heavily invested in the process (e.g., clinical faculty assigned to oversee the work of the triads). Be sure to bring to the meeting all existing documentation, especially that which refers to roles. Typically these documents are in the form of handbooks, print or virtual, created for each member of the triad. The meeting should begin with a brainstorming session in which each individual or group generates a list of roles and then compares those roles in practice with official roles listed in any gathered documents. This activity will determine current roles, as well as bring to light gaps and inconsistencies. Stakeholders should be encouraged to view the roles in both present and future. Where are we now and what can be improved?

5. Developing a Written Action Plan: After the roles for each member of the triad have been defined by the team, the communication plan can be written. Structures by which the triad will communicate with each other to ensure close collaboration is even more important than communicating out to centralized administration to ensure consistency, but both are necessary to consider in the stakeholder meeting. Obtaining feedback from stakeholders is imperative in order to determine to what extent the team has succeeded in clarifying roles, and what steps should be taken to address any issues.

   Communicating about roles on a regular basis is essential for the triad, and planning for this communication needs to follow the visit schedule for the university supervisor. If supervisor visits only occur a few times each semester, discussing roles may need to occur every visit. Communicating about roles within the larger group may need to occur only once per semester. Written follow-up may occur at the time of the larger meeting with multiple triads, or it may occur within the individual triads at a specified point or points in addition to occurring at a larger meeting. Again, planning for evaluation, formal or informal, is imperative.

6. Future Steps: If the team has set goals to clarify (and not make major changes to) triad roles, future steps may simply be to check in each semester as discussed above. However, if the team has planned significant changes for those roles, future steps might involve outlining several steps that meet that goal. For example, goals or role changes might be switching from face to face to virtual supervision, adding a person to the triad, switching to a coteaching model of student teaching, or adding formal or informal meetings between the student teacher and cooperating teacher for various purposes as described by the research. Those changes might need to be added step by step, or stakeholders might wish to clarify practices each semester before moving forward with planned changes in student teaching processes. As before, each step should be accompanied by opportunities for feedback from all parties.

7. Making Connections to Coursework: With respect to student teacher role clarity, making connections to coursework has benefits in both directions. By introducing roles for student teachers earlier in coursework, clarity will be enhanced. Making connections with previous fieldwork also benefits the entire program in terms of creating a developmental progression of roles in the field, from early fieldwork through student teaching. In this way, connections to coursework can start simple and continue to grow and reach back into early years in the preparation program.

MUTUAL PROFESSIONAL DEVELOPMENT

Mutual professional development is perhaps the most open-ended of the four principles presented in this book, when considered within the context of making change in student teaching. Traditionally, student teaching is viewed as a one-way street, with the benefits flowing from cooperating teacher to student teacher. Many cooperating teachers report side benefits from having a student teacher, but typically this type of learning appears to be informal and serendipitous. Mutual professional development simply means the creation of formal structures so that student teachers and cooperating teachers, and perhaps others inside or outside the triad, learn from one another.

1. Identify Stakeholders: The obvious stakeholders with whom to begin this work are members of the student teaching triad. A decision should be made early on as to whether to involve others such as faculty and administrators at K-12 schools and/or the university. Therefore, the first

question to ask is, who will benefit from the professional development? If wishing to start small, the answer may be simply, the student teachers and cooperating teachers, and then plan to expand from there. However, the school may be wishing to tap into different kinds of professional development that the university may be able to provide. An informal survey of partners might precede the meeting.

2. Outline Research Findings: For mutual professional development, the research does not come directly from research on student teaching, but rather from research on partnerships in support of teacher growth, both preservice and inservice. A good resource from which to gain information about professional development overall is Darling-Hammond and colleagues' Effective Teacher Professional Development, available from learningpolicyinstitute.org. This resource presents research-based elements of quality professional development and includes a section on Professional Learning Communities (PLCs). The Southwest Educational Development Laboratory also compiled guidelines for PLCs (http://www.sedl.org/pubs/change34/plc-cha34.pdf), which are more participatory and democratic than traditional professional development structures for teachers, making them ideal for use with a mutual model. Many reference guides for professional development can work here, as the basics should be similar (sustained work on mutually developed goals with careful evaluation and follow-through).

   A half-page summary will assist stakeholders in understanding the basics of quality professional development. Unfortunately, too few education professionals have been exposed to quality professional development. Therefore, taking the time to describe what works should be quite beneficial.

3. List Benefits: Benefits do not need to be sorted by stakeholders, because they are truly "mutual." The research and reports listed above identify the potential benefits for growth as professionals. Some research has tied quality professional development for practicing teachers to improved outcomes for youth, which of course is the ultimate goal for these plans.

4. Meeting of Stakeholders: Although the number and type of stakeholders may vary as discussed above, the meeting must include school administrators who oversee professional development. Ideally, the professional development planned should be aligned with the school's current professional development plan. The closer the alignment, the greater the benefit to individuals as well as to the school.

5. Developing a Written Action Plan: A professional development plan can range from very simple to very complex. For example, the student teacher could introduce new technology to the cooperating teacher, and

they would work together to determine how best to integrate the technology in the curriculum to benefit K-12 student learning. On the other end, university professors and student teachers could plan weekly or monthly professional development sessions addressing all of a building's teachers around a certain theme, for example, mental health supports or project-based learning. Teachers could then determine how to implement the initiative in their classroom with carefully planned evaluation and follow through. Student teachers could spend part of their time collaborating with other teachers, supporting them by assisting with data collection and analysis.

Rather than articulating principles, the Action Plan should involve a written description of the activities and evaluation, outlining specific roles and a timeline. The communication plan is also very important, particularly as the action plan may need to be communicated to individuals beyond the stakeholder group, for example, all teachers in a specific building. The communication plan will need administrator buy-in and continued support. The communication plan should be in writing and ensure a good fit with the professional roles of all stakeholders.

The communication plan also needs to include a thorough evaluation plan. Again, regardless of the size of the initiative, collecting formal or informal data on the plan's successes and challenges is imperative. If individuals did not follow through with the plans or change teaching practices to benefit K-12 students, why not? What can be improved? Often, insufficient time is allotted when planning for and implementing a new structure in teaching. Sustainability is a reason why alignment to curricular goals or even replacing some existing structures can be helpful.

6. Future Steps: In this case, future steps need to be determined after one iteration of the plan for mutual professional development, because what is considered "professional development" varies so widely and is challenging to implement with impact. Outcomes should be analyzed carefully, because too often we continue with the same professional development plans without attempting to determine impact. In this case, benefits need to be evaluated both for student teachers and cooperating teachers. If benefits are not seen, the team may need to take the data on what did not work and start over. Mutual professional development is possible and has the promise of powerful outcomes, but alignment with research-based principles and practical needs must occur.

7. Making Connections to Coursework: The most apparent connection to coursework is the specific theme of the professional development selected by the stakeholders. If the student teachers can go into the experience with knowledge of the curriculum, pedagogy or technology highlighted

by the partners, preparedness, and outcomes will be enhanced. The contributions and expertise of faculty can also be tapped both prior to and
during the student teaching experience. Greater involvement of student
teachers and faculty prior to student teaching will enhance partnerships
and contribute to growth in other ways.

Chapter 10

Planning for Innovation

The previous chapter discussed beginning the work of redesigning student teaching by starting small, targeting a single principle of the four described in chapter 8. This chapter presents innovation in a broader context, considering student teaching as the capstone experience in an entire teacher preparation program. Implementing even one of these four principles in student teaching will strengthen partnerships as well as the student teaching experience, and open possibilities for connections to both course- and fieldwork throughout the program. However, addressing each of the principles programmatically, in partnership with schools and districts in this context, can jump-start complete redesign and narrow the research-to-practice gap by connecting various program components and creating a developmental sequence of experiences, supported by coursework and culminating in student teaching. Looking into the future, the ultimate goal of reconstituting teacher preparation is to create a seamless system to transition teachers from preservice to inservice training and supports. The system will meet individual as well as partner goals, enhance teaching and learning, offer consistent and developmental supports, and set up new teachers to remain in the classroom and thrive as lifelong learners focused on student growth.

The work discussed in this chapter will connect each semester of course and fieldwork, rather than jumping directly to the student teaching experience. In considering the developmental progression of course and fieldwork, each of the other three principles can be incorporated to strengthen partnership and narrow the research-to-practice gap in teacher preparation. Student teaching will be addressed as a culminating experience in the program. Finally, the chapter will discuss one of the most crucial but rarely addressed components of teacher development: connecting the teacher preparation to the first year of teaching. In this chapter, following the principles in order is key, as they build on one another.

DEVELOPING A COMMON PHILOSOPHY

Developing a common philosophy to guide an entire program differs from developing a common philosophy just for student teaching, although the process is relatively similar. The primary difference is simply the variety of stakeholders included. Stakeholders would include all school partners, cooperating teachers and administrators, field placement personnel, university administrators, and all faculty in the various disciplines. Of particular importance is to include anyone who has shown interest in expanding partnerships. This team can get unwieldy, so in following the steps outlined in the previous chapter, you may need to utilize a two-level approach, one for broader strokes addressing larger goals, and a smaller committee to fill in the details. This approach allows everyone to have input but leaves the specifics for a more committed group that will guide the redesign process and continue involvement throughout implementation and evaluation. In following the steps described previously, "Future Steps" should include the remaining three principles from chapter 8 discussed below as they pertain to full program innovation.

Triad Role Clarity

The common philosophy will guide the remainder of the work in program redesign. The next principle to tackle is Triad Role Clarity, as it provides a foundation for the design of clinical experiences in the program. As originally proposed by the Blue Ribbon Panel in 2010, teacher preparation programs should layer coursework on top of carefully designed clinical experiences, rather than attempting to fit in the clinical experiences within an already-designed program of coursework. The triad should be considered in a broader sense, that is, teacher candidates—school personnel—college of education supervisors, so as to allow for consideration of and creativity with those "boundary spanners" identifying the "third spaces" in clinical education.

Just as with developing a common philosophy, more individuals will be involved in clarifying roles. Addressing this principle early on in the redesign process will pay off immensely, as role confusion has been related to stagnation in the student teaching progress (Valencia et al., 2009). Further clarifying roles provides this opportunity to consider teacher preparation programs as a whole rather than considering each semester or "block" separately.

Since Zeichner used the term "third space" in 2010 to refer to new opportunities to define roles connecting K-12 and teacher preparation / higher education, others have used "third space" in addition to "boundary spanners" to refer to the work of individuals defining the space bridging K-12 and teacher preparation. Unfortunately, much of the existing work in this area is either theoretical or a description of roles defined by a single partnership or university. As such, there is little, if any, comparative research on effective models or practices. The state of the professional literature in this area can be seen either as a challenge or an opportunity, in that partners can define or tailor the space to local needs, thus expanding creative options.

Again, simplicity is key. How can the common philosophy be applied to the various roles in the triad? What structures must change in course and fieldwork? There are several ways to conceptualize and organize this work:

1. Start with individuals already working as "Boundary Spanners" such as faculty liaisons, clinical faculty, and teaching supervisors in K-12 who have a significant amount of responsibility in both settings, and have them lead the re-envisioning process.
2. Use the smaller team that developed the common philosophy and ensure that it includes those most deeply involved or interested in partnership work.
3. If the goal is to replace current systems completely, put together a small team of partners in both K-12 and higher education who have not been involved in partnership work, such as individuals new to the organization. They may envision completely new work and roles for the partnership, based on the common philosophy.

Again, retaining simplicity and organization is a must. The use of focus groups and surveys can expand input from stakeholders in an effort to reach consensus. Your group may wish to focus initially on defining roles for "Boundary Spanners" before addressing the expanded triad. Out of all of these stakeholders, teacher candidates are most easily left out of the loop. Obtaining representation from the full range of the body of teacher candidates is very important, including nontraditional or struggling candidates, as well as those from underrepresented backgrounds.

Defining the scope of the work is very important. Which roles will be clarified and what will implementation look like? Who will oversee the process? You may wish to begin by relying on existing documents, or you may wish to start from scratch, particularly as such documents are developed over time and include multiple add-ons that may or may not apply to the current program structure.

You may also wish to begin by identifying existing problems with the triad in partnering schools and districts. Which roles are more or less clear and how should the work move forward? Linking with the common philosophy can assist in this process. Avoid falling into the following traps by reviewing them with the team:

1. Adding more language, rules or roles without replacing old ones;
2. Creating new roles and/or documents without plans for follow-through;
3. Not including or acknowledging all stakeholders;
4. Failing to share new philosophies or goals with all stakeholders;
5. Not considering what new roles will look like in practice, or what success will look like in practice;
6. Not supporting individuals in transition to new roles (i.e., providing professional development); or
7. Failing to set, enact, or follow-through with evaluation plans.

Of all of the above cautions, the last two may be of most importance. The need for solid support and evaluation is essential to ensuring lasting change and to understanding to what extent those changes have met intended goals.

MUTUAL PROFESSIONAL DEVELOPMENT

As stated above, role clarity with particular attention to defining "third spaces," will leave room for innovation. Mutual professional development is the opportunity to further define and personalize your "third space," as well as to connect with your new philosophy. Again, simplicity and organization are important to consider. An initial effort might look like one of the following:

1. Semiannual professional development events that include teachers, teacher candidates, and university faculty as co-learners
2. Inclusive study groups around a book, Lesson Study, or research project
3. An integrated action research project, designed to address a school or district goal and
4. Integrated child study teams

Any professional development efforts should relate both to the common philosophy and to K-12 learning, for example, Positive Behavior Intervention and Supports (PBIS), Project-Based Learning (PBL), or Culturally Responsive Teaching Practices (CRT). The work of rolling in professional development should start small, with plans to expand in future semesters and years. Expansion can include more individuals, more classrooms/grades/subjects/schools, and/or more intensive data collection.

However, evaluation data should be examined before plans for expansion are implemented. These plans can be outlined in the "Future Plans" section discussed above.

TARGETED MATCHMAKING

Targeted Matchmaking is the one principle that does apply primarily to student teaching, although it can be used for other clinical experiences as well. As discussed previously, the potential benefit of deliberate matchmaking is to increase the goodness of fit for student teachers, improve preparation for future positions, and increase future retention. Although the research in this area is still in its infancy, the results are quite compelling. Often, institutions of higher education make placements based on accreditation requirements; for example, teacher candidates must have rural and urban placements, placements at different grade levels or in various types of classrooms. The balance between teacher candidate preference and the need for breath and depth in clinical experience can be a challenge in teacher preparation; the research does not yet provide a solution.

In addition to student teaching, consider how teacher candidates are assigned to their clinical placements throughout the program. How can each member of the initial triad have more voice in this process? How can the balance between support and evaluation be addressed, as well as the balance between needs and desires of the teacher candidate? For example, a candidate might resist important types of field placements, such as ones that include specific types of diverse learners or grade levels that are part of the licensure structure. Matchmaking can also be informed by the plans created by the teams addressing the three other principles.

Traditionally, field placements have been one-sided. The district and university make a partnership that involves the district offering to provide some number of placements for teacher candidates, often recurring semesterly or annually. Typically, neither teacher quality nor goodness of fit between cooperating teacher and teacher candidates is considered. Most often, districts take charge of selecting cooperating teachers without the input of the university. School administrators and sometimes teacher unions determine the assignments (Greenberg et al., 2011).

Redesigning teacher education is an opportunity to rethink such automatic assignment and create new structures that are mutually beneficial. The following are examples of types of structures that partners might wish to consider:

1. Identify a desired developmental progression of field placements and matchmaking, from traditional matchmaking used for initial field

placements to in-depth interviewing by potential cooperating teachers and administrators to determine placements
2. Develop common procedures to be applied throughout placements
3. Establish "checkpoints" for teacher candidates at various points in the program, at which they are matched with teachers and districts based on data and
4. Appoint liaisons (from university or district) to work as mediators in placing teacher candidates with teachers and districts based on data, either for specific placements or for all placements in the program

Previous work around developing the common philosophy may assist with this process in terms of understanding goals and perspectives of partners. Often schools and universities do not see eye to eye with respect to what qualities make a good cooperating teacher and/or a good teacher candidate or match. Many traits that are typically considered and even required are unrelated to research outcomes, for example, master's degree requirements for cooperating teachers or a GPA requirement for teacher candidates. This question is further complicated by the fact that desirable traits are often difficult to measure (e.g., openness to learning, positive attitude) and are interpreted differently by different cultures, thus leaving the process open to considerable bias. Determining "look-fors" can guide the teacher preparation program's standards and content, also helping to solidify dispositions.

REDESIGN SUMMARY

Redesigning teacher education is not easy, particularly when conducted in partnership with district(s). The two institutions have different traditions, different standards, different goals, and different structures, including reward structures. However, when they are able to work together in harmony, everyone benefits. The challenge is to determine ways to collaborate that meet local needs and fit best practices and are achievable by people who are already handling a full plate.

This chapter on redesign begins with a discussion of how to develop a common philosophy with school partners in order to guide innovation. The philosophy should be learner-centered and simple and shared by all stakeholders. Determine what the philosophy looks like in practice, across K-12 and higher education, will be the major work of the team as the process of redesign unfolds. An iterative process will assist with the work, as coming back to the philosophy and related data on a regular basis will keep the work bounded and simpler to organize and explain.

After determining a common philosophy, the partners should clarify the roles of the triad. Considering these roles more broadly can solidify the "third spaces" needed for innovation. Teacher preparation programs should be built around a series of carefully designed clinical experiences rather than designing experiences around required coursework. Clarifying roles also sets expectations for the structure of the experiences and connects with the common philosophy, allowing the partners to define that philosophy through specific expectations and actions.

Mutual professional development is the next element to be addressed in the program design. After roles are clarified, partners will be able to determine the additional work needed to be able to meet the goals identified by the partnership. For example, through their work, partners might identify a need for training in PBIS, or mental health supports, or math intervention. Mutual professional development can further connect the partners by using new structures and channels to develop new support systems. Identifying needs can inform coursework and transform faculty's teaching, research, and service through action research and new structures for teaching and research. Solid evaluation and analysis of data collected are key to moving forward and determine effectiveness of the redesign effort.

Targeted matchmaking is the final element to consider, connecting the work of the partners through the deliberate placement of teacher candidates with particular cooperating teachers in particular schools. When roles are defined and professional development needs met, matchmaking can maximize outcomes of these efforts. New research is showing that the impact of such matchmaking can provide returns will beyond the single placement semester or year. Districts benefit in obtaining a first look or "extended interview" of teacher candidates they may wish to hire in the future, as well as an opportunity to orient them to the specific context in which they may be working later. This experience represents a significant boost in transitioning into the first year or years of teaching.

INTO THE FUTURE

One of the least explored but most promising opportunities in teacher preparation is the transition from student teaching to the first year of teaching. Because of the traditional separate systems approach to preservice and inservice education/continuing professional development, plus the different funding approaches that support each type of training, few if any supports are typically put into place to guide teachers from the student teaching experience into their first teaching assignment. These systems offer different supports and which often emphasize different teaching and learning goals. This disconnect between preparation and practice during the teachers' formative education further exacerbates the issues presented above (Zeichner, 2018).

The research literature on teacher induction is helpful but not always encouraging. The connection between preservice and inservice training is typically nonexistent, and teachers must transition between two support systems that appear to have little in common, in terms of goals, processes, documentation, and follow-through. Quality teacher induction programs can lead to enhanced teacher quality, but many of these programs are time- and resource-intensive, and still lack connection with previous training (Ingersoll, 2012). An opportunity that is wide open for higher education/district partnerships is to design, implement, and evaluate a seamless support system that connects preservice and inservice preparation. Such systems must be intensive, supportive, personalized, and focused on the needs of local K-12 students (Zeichner, 2018).

Thus, the next step is to define, create, implement and evaluate bridges that connect student teaching goals and supports to those offered during the first years of teaching (induction) and beyond to continuing professional development within local contexts. The principles presented in this book can lead to a smooth transition from preparation to practice, whether teacher candidates take teaching positions in the student teaching district or a related district. However, the challenge for the future is to determine how nurture and sustain this connection, so every new teacher understands his/her role, is supported by his/her teacher preparation program, school and district, and has opportunities for ongoing connected, personalized growth, supported by trained personnel.

References

AACTE. (2010). *The clinical preparation of teachers: A policy brief*. Washington, D.C.: Author.

AACTE. (2018a). *A pivot toward clinical practice, its lexicon, and the renewal of educator preparation*. Washington, D.C.: Author.

AACTE. (2018b). *Colleges of education: A national portrait*. Washington, D.C.: Author.

Allen, D. S., Perl, M., Goodson, L., & Sprouse, T. (2014). Changing traditions: Supervision, co-teaching, and lessons learned in a professional development school partnership. *Educational Considerations, 42*(1), 19–29.

Anderson, J. D. (1988). *The education of Blacks in the South 1860–1935*. Chapel Hill, NC: University of North Carolina.

Andrews, L. O. (1964). *Student teaching*. New York: Center for Applied Research in Education.

Appleberry, M. (1976). What did you learn from student teaching? *Instructor, 8*(6), 38–40.

Arends, R. I. (2006). Performance assessment in perspective: History, opportunities, and challenges. In S. Castle & B. D. Shaklee (Eds.), *Assessing teacher performance: Performance-based assessment in teacher education* (pp. 3–22). Lanham, MD: Rowman & Littlefield.

Arnett-Hartwick, S. E. (2015). A qualitative study of the student teaching time frame. *Journal of Family and Consumer Sciences Education, 32*(1), 42–48.

Bacharach, N., Heck, T. W., & Dahlberg, K. (2010). Changing the face of student teaching through co-teaching. *Action in Teacher Education, 32*, 3–14.

Bachevich, A., Dodman, S. L., Hall, L., & Ludwig, M. (2015). Building a research agenda and developing solutions for challenges in clinical experiences. In E. R. Hollins (Ed.), *Rethinking field experiences in preservice teacher preparation* (pp. 202–221). New York: Routledge.

Baeton, M., & Simons, M. (2016). Innovative field experiences in teacher education: Student-teachers and mentors as partners in education. *International Journal of Teaching and Learning in Higher Education, 28*(1), 38–51.

Barnes, H. L. (1987). The conceptual basis for thematic teacher education programs. *Journal of Teacher Education, 38*(4), 13–18.

Billingsley, G. M., & Scheuermann, B. K. (2014). Using virtual technology to enhance field experiences for pre-service special education teachers. *Teacher Education and Special Education, 37*(3), 255–272.

Blanton, L., McLeskey, J., & Taylor, K. H. (2014). Examining indicators of teacher education program quality: Intersections between general and special education. In P. T. Sindelar, E. D. McCray, M. T. Brownell, & B. Lignugaris/Kraft (Eds.), *Handbook of research on special education teacher preparation* (pp. 129–142). New York: Routledge.

Borrowman, M. L. (1956). *The liberal and technical in teacher education*. New York: Teachers College, Columbia University.

Borrowman, M. L. (1975). About teachers of education. In A. Bagley (Ed.), *The professor of education: An assessment of conditions* (pp. 55–60). Minneapolis, MN: Society of Professors of Education.

Boyd, D., Grossman, P., Lankford, H., Loeb, S. I., & Wyckoff, J. (2009). Teacher preparation and student achievement. *Educational Evaluation and Policy Analysis, 30*(4), 319–343.

Breault, R., & Breault, D. A. (2012). *Professional development schools: Researching lessons from the field*. Lanham, MA: Rowman & Littlefield.

Breault, R. A., & Lack, B. (2009). Equity and empowerment in PDS work: A review of literature (1999 to 2006). *Equity and Excellence in Education, 42*(2), 152–168.

Burke, W. I. (1978). Teacher centers: Cooperative endeavors. *High School Journal, 61*, 150–161.

Burns, R. W., Jacobs, J., & Yendol-Hoppey, D. (2016). The changing nature of the role of the university supervisor and function of preservice teacher supervision in an era of clinically-rich practice. *Action in Teacher Education, 38*(4), 410–425.

Buttery, T. J., Guyton, E., & Sikula, J. P. (1996). *Handbook of research on teacher education* (2nd ed.). New York: MacMillan.

Butts, R. F. (1978). *Public education in the United States: From revolution to reform*. New York: Holt, Rinehart and Winston.

Butts, R. F., & Cremin, L. A. (1953). *A history of education in American culture*. New York: Holt, Rinehart and Winston.

Cherian, F. (2007). Learning to teach: Teacher candidates reflect on the relational, conceptual, and contextual influences of responsive mentorship. *Canadian Journal of Education, 30*(1), 25–46.

Chetty, R., Friedman, J., & Rockoff, J. (2014). Measuring the impacts of teachers II: Teacher value-added and student outcome in adulthood. *American Economic Review, 104*, 2633–2679.

Chung, R. R. (2008). Beyond assessment: Performance assessment. *Teacher Education Quarterly, 35*(11), 7–28.

Clifford, G. J. (1986). The formative years of schools of education in America: A five-institution analysis. *American Journal of Education, 94*(4), 427–446.

Clifford, G. J., & Guthrie, J. W. (1988). *Ed school.* Chicago: University of Chicago Press.

Clift, R. T., & Brady, P. (2005). Research on methods courses and field experiences. In M. C. Smith & K. M. Zeichner (Eds.), *Studying teacher education: The report of the AERA panel on research and teacher education.* Mahweh, NJ: Lawrence Erlbaum.

Cochran-Smith, M. (1991). Reinventing student teaching. *Journal of Teacher Education, 42*(2), 104–118.

Cochran-Smith, M. (2004). The problem of teacher education. *Journal of Teacher Education, 55*(4), 295–299.

Cochran-Smith, M., & Fries, K. (2005). Researching teacher education in changing times: Politics and paradigms. In M. Cochran-Smith & K. M. Zeichner (Eds.), *Studying teacher education: The report of the AERA panel on research and teacher education.* Mahwah, NJ: Lawrence Erlbaum.

Cochran-Smith, M., & Zeichner, K. M. (Eds.). (2005). *Studying teacher education: The report of the AERA panel on research and teacher education.* Mahweh, NJ: Lawrence Erlbaum.

Conant, J. B. (1964). *The education of American teachers.* New York: McGraw-Hill.

Council for the Accreditation of Educator Preparation. (2013). *CAEP 2013: Standards for the accreditation of educator preparation.* Washington, D.C.: Author.

Council of Chief State School Officers. (2012). *Our responsibility, our promise: Transforming educator preparation and entry into the profession.* Washington, D.C.: Author.

Cremin, L. A. (1957). *The republic and the school: Horace Mann on the education of free men.* New York: Teachers College.

Cuban, L. (1984). *How teachers taught: Constancy and change in American classrooms.* New York: Longman.

Darling-Hammond, L. (2012). *Powerful teacher education lessons from exemplary programs.* Hoboken, NJ: John Wiley.

Darling-Hammond, L., Hyler, M. E., & Gardner, M. (2017). *Effective teacher professional development.* Palo Alto, CA: Learning Policy Institute.

Edelfelt, R. A., & Raths, J. D. (1998). *A brief history of standards in teacher education.* Reston, VA: Association of Teacher Educators.

Elsbree, W. S. (1939). *The American teacher: Evolution of a profession in a democracy.* New York: American Book Company.

Farkas, S., & Duffett, A. (2011). *Cracks in the ivory tower: The views of education professors circa 2010.* Columbus, OH: Fordham Foundation. Retrieved from edexcellence.net.

Feiman-Nemser, S., & Buchmann, M. (1987). When is student teaching teacher education? *Teaching and Teacher Education, 3*(4), 255–273.

Fives, H., Hamman, D., & Olivarez, A. (2007). Does burnout begin with student teaching? Analyzing efficacy, burnout, and support during the student teaching semester. *Teaching and Teacher Education, 23*, 916–934.

Friend, M., Embury, D. C., & Clarke, L. (2015). Co-teaching versus apprentice teaching: An analysis of similarities and differences. *Teacher Education and Special Education, 38*(2), 79–87.

Glazer, N. (1974). The schools of the minor professions. *Minerva, 12*(3), 346–364.

Goldhaber, D., Krieg, J., Naito, N., & Theobald, R. (2019). *Student teaching and the geography of teacher shortages.* Washington, D.C.: CALDER Center Working Paper No. 222-1019.

Goldhaber, D., Krieg, J., & Theobald, R. (2018). *Exploring the impact of student teaching apprenticeships on student achievement and mentor teachers.* CEDR Working Paper No. 11222018-1-1. Seattle, WA: University of Washington.

Goldhaber, D., Krieg, J. M., & Theobald, R. (2017). Does the match matter? Exploring whether student teaching experiences affect teacher effectiveness. *American Educational Research Journal, 54*(2), 325–359.

Greenberg, J., Pomerance, L., & Walsh, K. (2011). *Student teaching in the United States.* Washington, D.C.: National Council on Teacher Quality.

Grew, R., & Harrigan, S. (1990). *The development of a national system of education in France.* Ann Arbor: University of Michigan Press.

Guyton, E., & McIntyre, D. J. (1990). Student teaching and school experiences. In W. R. Houston (Ed.), *Handbook of research on teacher education* (pp. 514–534). New York: Macmillan.

Haj-Broussard, M., Husbands, J. L., Dunnick Karge, B., McAlister, K. W., McCabe, M., Omelan, J. A., & Stephens, C. (2015). Clinical prototypes: Nontraditional teacher preparation programs. In E. R. Hollins (Ed.), *Rethinking field experiences in preservice teacher preparation* (pp. 70–92). New York: Routledge.

Hall, S. R. (1829). *Lectures on school-keeping.* Boston: Richardson, Lord and Halbrook.

Haring, M., & Nelson, E. (1980). A five year follow-up comparison of recent and experienced graduates from campus and field based teacher education programs. Paper presented at the annual meeting of the American Educational Research Association, Boston, MA.

Harper, C. (1939). *A century of public teacher education.* Washington, D.C.: American Association of Teachers Colleges.

Harper, C. A. (1935). *Development of teachers colleges in the United States.* Bloomington, IL: McKnight and McKnight.

Harper, C. A. (1939). *A century of public teacher education.* Trenton, NJ: National Education Association of America.

Harper, E. (2010). Dame Schools. In *Encyclopedia of educational reform and dissent* (pp. 259–260). Beverly Hills, CA: Sage Publications.

Harris, D., & Sass, T. (2011). Teacher training, teacher quality and student achievement. *Journal of Public Economics, 95*(7), 798–812.

Herbst, J. (1966). *The once and future school: Three hundred and fifty years of American public education.* New York: Routledge.

Herbst, J. (1980). Beyond the debates over revisionism: Three educational pasts writ lar. *History of Education Quarterly, 20*, 131–145.

Hess, M. B. (1971). The student teaching center: Filling the new order in student teaching. *The Journal of Teacher Education, 22*(3), 299–302.

Hirsch, E. D., Jr. (1996). *The schools we need and why we need them.* New York: Anchor Books.

Hixon, E., & So, H.-J. (2009). Technology's role in field experiences for preservice teacher training. *Educational Technology & Society, 12*(4), 294–304.

Hoffman, J. V., Wetzel, M. M., Maloch, B., Greeter, E., Taylor, L., DeJulio, S., & Vlach, S. K. (2015). What can we learn from studying the coaching interactions between cooperating teachers and preservice teachers? A literature review. *Teaching and Teacher Education, 52*, 99–112.

Hollins, E. R. (2015). *Rethinking field experiences in preservice teacher preparation.* New York: Routledge.

Holmes Group. (1986). *Tomorrow's teachers: A report of the Holmes Group.* East Lansing, MI (501 Erickson Hall, East Lansing 48824-1034): Holmes Group.

Houston, W. R., Haberman, M., & Sikula, J. (1990). *Handbook of research on teacher education.* New York: MacMillan.

Hoy, W. K., & Rees, R. (1977). The bureaucratic socialization of student teachers. *Journal of Teacher Education, 28*(1), 23–26.

Imig, D., Wiseman, D., & Imig, S. (2011). Teacher education in the United States of America, 2011. *Journal of Education for Teaching, 37*(4), 399–408.

Ingersoll, R. (2012). Beginning teacher induction: What the data tell us. *Phi Delta Kappan, 93*(8), 47–51.

Johnson, I. L., & Napper-Owen, G. (2011). The importance of role perceptions in the student teaching triad. *Physical Educator, 68*(1), 44–56.

Johnson, J. A. (1968a). *A brief history of student teaching.* DeKalb, IL: Creative Education Materials.

Johnson, J. A. (1968b). *A national survey of student teaching programs: Final report.* Dekalb, IL: Northern Illinois University.

Joint Committee on State Responsibility for Student Teaching. (1966). *Who's in charge here? Fixing responsibilities for student teaching.* Washington, D.C.: National Commission on Teacher Education and Professional Standards.

Joint Committee on State Responsibility for Student Teaching. (1967). *A new order in student teaching: Fixing responsibilities for student teaching.* Washington, D.C.: National Commission on Teacher Education and Professional Standards.

Karabel, J. (2005). *The chosen: The hidden story of admission and exclusion at Harvard, Yale and Princeton.* Boston: Houghton Mifflin.

Koerner, J. D. (1963). *The miseducation of American teachers.* Boston: Houghton Mifflin.

Krieg, J. M., Theobald, R., & Goldhaber, D. (2016). A foot in the door: Exploring the role of student teaching assignments in teachers' initial job placements. *Educational Evaluation and Policy Analysis, 38*(2), 364–388.

Labaree, D. F. (2006). *The trouble with ed schools.* New Haven, CT: Yale University Press.

Lane, K. L., Menzies, H. M., Ennis, R. P., & Bezdek, J. (2013). School-wide systems to promote positive behaviors and facilitate instruction. *Journal of Curriculum and Instruction, 7*(1), 6–31.

Levine, A. (2006). Educating school teachers: The education schools project. Retrieved from edschools.org.

Lipset, S. M., & E. Raab. (1970). *The politics of unreason*. New York: Harper and Row.

Littleton, MA School Committee. (1849). Quoted in "only a teacher: Teaching timeline". Retrieved from http://www.pbs.org/onlyteacher/timeline.html.

Liu, K., Miller, R., Dickmann, E., & Monday, K. (2018). Virtual supervision of student teachers as a catalyst for educational equity in rural areas. *Journal of Formative Design in Learning*, 2(1), 8–19.

Lucas, C. J. (1997). *Teacher education in America*. New York: St. Martin's Press.

Maheady, L., Smith, C., & Jabot, M. (2014). Field experiences and instructional pedagogies in teacher education: What we know, don't know, and must learn soon. In P. T. Sindelar, E. D. McCray, M. T. Brownell, & B. Lignugaris/Kraft (Eds.), *Handbook of research on special education teacher preparation* (pp. 161–177). New York: Routledge.

McMaster, J. B. (1910). *A history of the people of the United States: From the revolution to the civil war*. New York: D. Appleton and Company.

National Commission on Teaching and America's Future. (1996). *What matters most: Teaching for America's future*. New York: National Commission on Teaching and America's Future.

National Council for Accreditation of Teacher Education. (2010). *Transforming teacher education through clinical practice: A national strategy to prepare effective teachers*. Washington, D.C.: National Council for Accreditation of Teacher Education.

National Council for the Accreditation of Teacher Education. (2001). *Standards for professional development schools*. Washington, D.C.: Author.

No Child Left Behind Act of 2001, P.L. 107-110, 20 U.S.C. § 6319. (2002).

Nosow, S. (1975). Students' perceptions of field experience education. *Journal of College Student Personnel*, 16(6), 508–513.

Odom, S. L., Brantlinger, E., Gersten, R., Horner, R. H., Thompson, B., & Harris, K. R. (2005). Research in special education: Scientific methods and evidence-based practices. *Exceptional Children*, 71, 137–148.

Orazum, P. F. (1987). Black-white differences in schooling: Investment and human capital. *American Economic Review*, 77(4), 714–723.

Pangburn, J. M. (1932). *The education of teachers college*. New York: Columbia University.

Parker, M. H. (1954). Some educational activities of the Freedman's Bureau. *Journal of Negro Education*, 23(1), 9–21.

Perlmann, J., & Margo, R. (2001). *Women's work? American school teachers 1650–1970*. Chicago: University of Chicago Press.

Peseau, B. A. (1990). Financing teacher education. In W. R. Houston (Ed.), *Handbook of research on teacher education* (pp. 157–172). New York: Macmillan.

Pierce, T. (1955). *White and Negro schools in the south: An analysis of biracial education*. Englewood Cliffs, NJ: Prentice Hall.

Ravitch, D. (2003). *A brief history of teacher professionalism*. White House conference on preparing tomorrow's teachers. Washington, D.C.: U.S. Department of Education.

Rock, M. L., Gregg, M., Thead, B. K., Acker, S. E., Gable, R. A., & Zigmond, N. P. (2009). Can you hear me now? Evaluation of an online wireless technology to provide real-time feedback to special education teachers-in-training. *Teacher Education and Special Education, 32*(1), 64–82.

Ronfeldt, M. (2012). Where should student teachers learn to teach? Effects of field placement school characteristics on teacher retention and effectiveness. *Educational Evaluation and Policy Analysis, 34*(1), 3–26.

Ronfeldt, M. (2015). Field placement schools and instructional effectiveness. *Journal of Teacher Education, 66*(4), 304–320.

Ronfeldt, M., Matsko, K. K., Greene Nolan, H., & Reininger, M. (2018). *Who knows if our teachers are prepared? Three different perspectives on graduates' instructional readiness and the features of preservice preparation that predict them.* CEPA Working Paper No. 18-01. Stanford Center for Education Policy Analysis.

Ronfeldt, M., & Reiniger, M. (2012). More or better student teaching? *Teaching and Teacher Education, 28,* 1091–1106.

Rust, F. L., & Clift, R. T. (2015). Moving from recommendations to action in preparing professional educators. In E. R. Hollins (Ed.), *Rethinking field experiences in preservice teacher preparation* (pp. 47–69). New York: Routledge.

Schaefer, J. M., & Ottley, J. R. (2018). Evaluating immediate feedback via bug-in-ear as evidence-based practice for professional development. *Journal of Special Education Technology, 33*(4), 247–258.

Scheeler, M. C., Bruno, K., Grubb, E., & Seavey, T. L. (2009). Generalizing teaching techniques from university to K-12 classrooms: Teaching preservice teachers to use what they learn. *Journal of Behavioral Education, 18*(3), 189–210.

Scheeler, M. C., Ruhl, K. L., & McAfee, J. K. (2004). Providing performance feedback to teachers: A review. *Teacher Education and Special Education, 27*(4), 396–407.

Schmidt, M., Gage, A. M., Gage, N., Cox, P., & McLeskey, J. (2015). Bringing the field to the supervisor: Innovation in distance supervision for field-based using mobile technologies. *Rural Special Education Quarterly, 34*(1), 37–43.

Schmieder, A. A., & Yarger, S. J. (1974). Teacher/teacher centering in America. *Journal of Teacher Education, 25*(1), 5–12.

Schneider, J. (2018). Marching forward, marching in circles: A history of problems and dilemmas in teacher preparation. *Journal of Teacher Education, 64*(4), 330–340.

Schwartz-Bechet, B. (2014). Virtual supervision of teacher candidates: A case study. *The International Journal of Learning: Annual Review, 21.* Common Ground.

Segura Pirtle, S., & Tobia, E. (2014). Implementing effective professional learning communities. *SEDL Insights, 2*(3).

Sindelar, P. T., Wasburn-Moses, L., Casey, R. A., & Leko, C. D. (2014). Teacher education and its current policy and economic contexts. In P. T. Sindelar, E. D. McCray, M. T. Brownell, & B. Lignugaris/Kraft (Eds.), *Handbook of research on special education teacher preparation* (pp. 3–16). New York: Routledge.

Small, S. E. (1979). The Yankee schoolmarm in Freemen's Schools: An analysis of attitudes. *Journal of Southern History, 45*(3), 381–402.

Smith, E. (1974). The state of the states in teacher centering. *Journal of Teacher Education, 25*(1), 2.

Soslau, E., Gallo-Fox, J., & Scantelbury, K. (2019). The promises and realities of implementing a coteaching model of student teaching. *Journal of Teacher Education, 70*(3), 265–279.

Spooner, M., Flowers, C., Lambert, R., & Algozzine, B. (2008). Is more really better? Examining perceived benefits of an extended student teaching experience. *The Clearing House, 81*(6), 263–270.

Steadman, S. C., & Brown, S. D. (2011). Defining the job of university supervisor: A department-wide study of university supervisors' practices. *Issues in Teacher Education, 20*(1), 51–68.

Stillman, J., Ragusa, G., & Whittaker, A. (2015). Teacher performance assessment: Readiness for professional practice. In E. R. Hollins (Ed.), *Rethinking field experiences in preservice teacher preparation* (pp. 171–201). New York: Routledge.

Stillwaggon, J. (2012). The Old Deluder, educational salvation and the limits of distributive justice. *Policy Futures in Education, 10*(3), 352–362.

Stowe, C. E. (1836). *The Prussian system of public instruction and its applicability to the United States.* Cincinnati, OH: Truman and Smith.

Stowe, C. E. (1838). *Report on elementary public instruction in Europe.* Harrisburg, PA: Packer, Barrett and Parke.

Travers, P. D. (1969). Calvin Ellis Hall and the history of education. *Peabody Journal of Education, 47*(2), 83–87.

Tyack, D. B. (1967). *Turning points in American educational history.* Waitham, MA: Blaisdell.

Urban, W. J. (1990a). Historical studies of teacher education. In W. R. Houston (Ed.), *Handbook of teacher education* (pp. 59–71). New York: Macmillan.

Urban, W. J. (1990b). Historical studies of teacher education. In W. R. Houston (Ed.), *Handbook of research on teacher education* (pp. 59–71). New York: Macmillan.

Valencia, S. W., Martin, S. D., Place, N. A., & Grossman, P. (2009). Complex interactions in student teaching: Lost opportunities for learning. *Journal of Teacher Education, 60*(3), 304–322.

Walk, G. E. (1917). Practice teaching and observation in normal schools. *Education, 38*, 69–85.

Walker, V. S., & Archung, K. N. (2003). The segregated schooling of Blacks in the United States and South Africa. *Comparative Education Review, 47*(1), 21–40.

Wasburn-Moses, L. (2017). A national descriptive survey of teacher residency programs. *School University Partnerships, 10*(2), 33–41.

Watts, D. (1987). Student teaching. In M. Haberman & J. M. Backus (Eds.), *Advances in teacher education* (pp. 151–167). Norwood, NJ: Ablex.

Williams, J. (2014). Teacher educator professional learning in the third space: Implications for identity and practice. *Journal of Teacher Education, 65*(4), 315–326.

Wilson, S., & Youngs, P. (2005). Research on accountability processes in teacher education. In M. Cochran-Smith & K. M. Zeichner (Eds.), *Studying teacher education: The report of the AERA panel on research and teacher education* (pp. 591–644). Mahweh, NJ: Lawrence Erlbaum.

Wilson, S. M., Floden, R. E., & Ferrini-Mundy, J. (2001). *Teacher preparation research: Current knowledge, gaps, and recommendations.* East Lansing, MI: Center for the Study of Teaching and Policy.

Wyman, A. (1995). The Earliest childhood teachers: Women teachers in America's Dame Schools. *Young Children, 50*(2), 29–32.

Yarger, S. J., & Leonard, A. (1974). *A descriptive and analytical study of the Teaching Center movement in American education.* Washington, D.C.: United States Office of Career Education.

Zeichner, K. (2002). Beyond traditional structures of student teaching. *Teacher Education Quarterly, 29*(2), 59–64.

Zeichner, K. M. (2010). Rethinking the connections between campus courses and field experiences in college- and university-based teacher education. *Journal of Teacher Education, 61*(1–2), 89–99.

Zeichner, K. M. (Ed.). (2018). *The struggle for the soul of teacher education.* New York: Routledge.

Zeichner, K. M., & Bier, M. (2018). Opportunities and pitfalls in the turn toward clinical experience in U.S. teacher education. In K. M. Zeichner (Ed.), *The struggle for the soul of teacher education* (pp. 197–223). New York: Routledge.

Zeichner, K. M., & Tabachnick, B. R. (1981). Are the effects of university teacher education 'washed out' by school experience? *Journal of Teacher Education, 32*(3), 7–11.

Zenkov, K., Corrigan, D. G., Beebe, R. S., & Sell, C. R. (Eds.). (2013). *Professional development schools and social justice.* Lanham, MA: Lexington.

Index

About the Authors

Leah Wasburn-Moses is professor of educational psychology at Miami University in Oxford, Ohio. Her areas of interest include innovation in teacher preparation, particularly with respect to teaching diverse learners, and the development of practical clinical partnerships. She has published four books, primarily in the area of teacher preparation. Her Campus Mentors (campusmentors.org) partnership model, a single-room alternative school located on a college campus, has won national awards for positive youth outcomes.

Philo C. Wasburn is professor emeritus of sociology at Purdue University, where he was an active faculty member from 1968 until 2012. His areas of interest include political sociology, with an emphasis on the role of communication in political life; socialization, with an emphasis on the school and the media as agents of political socialization; mass communication, with an emphasis on news and propaganda. He has published five books on these topics, as well as articles appearing in journals such as *Social Forces*; *Political Communication*; *Media, Culture and Society*; and the *Sociological Quarterly*.